"Eric knows firsthand the confusion, questions, pain, and emotions that can be associated with miscarriage. He writes of the hope that held and comforted him... and still does. *Ours* is theologically rich and offers wisdom, hope, comfort, and healing for men grieving miscarriage. A must-have for clergy too."

Rev. Dr. Justin S. Holcomb, Episcopal Minister; Seminary Professor

"Miscarriage affects couples, not just mothers. Men convince themselves that they need to be the strong ones and muscle on unaffected. Not so. Eric's tour of Luke's Gospel draws out pastoral applications which show real men how to grieve, care, love, grow, and understand following the tragedy of a miscarriage. There's nothing else like this book for men."

Adrian Reynolds, Head of National Ministries (UK), FIEC

"A one-of-a-kind resource. These honest reflections ask real questions and provide biblical hope in the midst of suffering. This is a must-read for grieving fathers as they process trauma and loss."

Emily Jensen and Laura Wifler, Co-founders, Risen Motherhood

"A masterclass for this as well as every other kind of grief. Scripture speaks of how those who have received comfort from Christ in their own sorrows are then able to bring comfort to others in theirs. *Ours* is a shining example of that reality."

Scott Sauls, Senior Pastor, Christ Presbyterian Church

"I do not wish anyone would need a book like this, but I do not doubt that many men will find it helpful during times of confusion, grief, and despair when tragedy strikes."

Rev. Dr. Michael F. Bird, Dean and Lecturer, Ridley College, Melbourne

"When we had our miscarriage we were crushed and confused. We did not know how to grieve, or even if we should grieve. I wish I'd had *Ours* at that time."

Ed Stetzer, Dean and Professor, Wheaton College

"Eric Schumacher comes alongside the grieving with a voice that is as theologically astute as it is tender. It's a book I wish my husband had had when we experienced our losses, and a book I am so grateful to be able to press into the hands of others."

Jasmine Holmes, Author, *Mother to Son*

"A profound, helpful book for men walking through great loss. I would recommend it not just to men who are grieving a miscarriage but to anyone who wants to be a better friend for them—and indeed, to anyone who wants to be more of a friend of Jesus."

Andy Crouch, Author, *Strong and Weak* and *The Tech-Wise Family*

"It is a number of years since my wife and I lost a child through miscarriage, and yet I still found Eric's book deeply comforting. In this particular and peculiar grief we need to see Jesus Christ in all his close compassion, costly love and kind sovereignty; and it is to Christ that Eric takes us daily. I unreservedly recommend this book."

John Hindley, Author, *Dealing with Disappointment*

"Imagine if, upon learning of your experience with miscarriage, a wise pastor who had suffered similar grief devoted an entire month to caring for you, opening the word of God with you, and helping your tired mind apply it to your questions, doubts, and shame. That's what Eric has done in this deeply pastoral, unwaveringly biblical, mercifully candid, and incredibly insightful devotional."

Abbey Wedgeworth, Author, *Held*

"Finally—a book that deals with the grief experienced by fathers who have lost children to miscarriage. This book will help men to grieve with hope and to minister to their wives and families at the same time. It is honest, biblical, practical, and timely."

Russell Moore, Author, *The Storm-Tossed Family*

"This is the devotional I wish someone had given to my husband when we went through our miscarriage. It's so good. So needed. So important. So tender. Eric named so many unnamed things."

Christine Caine, Founder, Propel Women

"This is the only book I have ever seen that is written for the father of a miscarried child. And it's a great one. Dig in, allow God to meet you in the pages of this book, and you will find healing and comfort. And share it with every dad you know."

Dave and Ann Wilson, Co-hosts, FamilyLife Today

ERIC SCHUMACHER

OURS

Biblical Comfort for Men
Grieving Miscarriage

Ours
© Eric Schumacher, 2022

Published by:
The Good Book Company

thegoodbook.com | thegoodbook.co.uk
thegoodbook.com.au | thegoodbook.co.nz | thegoodbook.co.in

ISBN: 9781784987282 | Printed in Turkey

Design by André Parker

Contents

To Dad,
who taught me to talk
about hard things

This book has a companion, written especially
for women: *Held: 31 Biblical Reflections on God's
Comfort and Care in the Sorrow of Miscarriage.*
Author Abbey Wedgeworth walks alongside readers
who are experiencing the heartbreak of pregnancy
loss, using Psalm 139 to help grieving mothers to
find comfort, assurance, and purpose.

Foreword

There will be a day when every child of God will be invited to the one funeral that we will all want to attend: we will be invited to the funeral of death. Yes, it really is true—death will die and eternally be no more. Along with it will die all the grief, pain, fear, sadness, suffering, and loss that death always drags with it. The completely righteous life of Jesus, the acceptable sacrifice of Jesus, and the victorious resurrection of Jesus, all accomplished on our behalf, guarantee that the enemy of everyone living—death—will finally and forever die. This is a wonderful hope for every child of God to hold on to.

But if you're a man dealing with the horrible shock and sadness of miscarriage, you know that we're not there yet. You and I still wake up every morning in a place where death is a dark reality that casts a fearful shadow over us. We all know that somehow, someway, death will burst through our door and shatter the safety of our most intimate places. Death is always hard, but the death of an infant occupies a category of its own. We sort of expect elderly loved ones to die someday; it is hard to let go of them, but their passing is not beyond the realm of our expectations. But the death of a child still in the womb seems particularly strange and irrational. Babies aren't supposed to die. How is it that life is allowed to grow in the womb, only to be snatched away before life outside the womb is ever given a chance to begin? Death is always hard, but a miscarriage just seems senseless to us.

So, when you face a miscarriage, there is something fundamental to understand. You won't just suffer the miscarriage, but you will also suffer how you suffer the miscarriage. We never come to these shocking and sad moments of life empty-handed. We always carry into them ways of thinking about God, ourselves, life's meaning and purpose, hardship, and what God has promised us, which will shape how we experience the painful thing we've gone through or are now going through. Wrong thinking always deepens the effects of already painful experiences. This is why the book you are about to read is so important and helpful.

But there is more. Being a man who is suffering through miscarriage brings with it a set of seductive, hard-to-resist temptations. Perhaps for you, it is anger, bringing God into the court of your judgment and questioning his goodness and love. Maybe it's the temptation to numb yourself in some way from the pain using busyness, media, chemical substances, or food. Perhaps for you, life seems unpredictable and dangerous in new ways, and you're tempted to give way to fear. Or maybe you're tempted to cope by denying the emotional, spiritual, and relational toll that miscarriage has taken on you. Perhaps for you, the temptation is envy: to be bitter as you see others enjoying what has been taken away from you. None of these things will produce a good harvest in your heart or your marriage, and all of them will make your suffering even more painful. In my time of loss, I think I have fallen into all of these temptations in some way.

You may be thinking, "Ok, Paul, I am struggling; where can I find help?" My immediate answer to that question is the book you are about to read. This book is a fountain of help for any man going through the dark valley of miscarriage. Let me tell you why.

First, Eric Schumacher understands that biblical faith—that is, trust that is rooted in God and his work on our behalf—will never ask you to deny reality. If you deny the reality of what you have gone through or are going through, you may achieve some temporary peace, but you're not experiencing the full healing power of biblical faith. This book is written by a man who has walked through the dark valley of miscarriage again and again. So, the painful realities of its hardship and loss splash across page after page. If you're a man dealing with the emotional, spiritual, and relational trauma of miscarriage, you will find yourself in this book, and you will come to understand your experience of loss more fully and deeply. But even more importantly, you will realize more fully, maybe more than ever before, that God understands every aspect of your suffering, and because he does, he is never put off or disgusted by what you are going through.

You can bring your anguish to him and find mercy and grace form-fitted for that particular moment of need.

There is a second and even more glorious theme in this book. This theme is why I will recommend what Eric has written here again and again. He has come to understand that when we are suffering, God's greatest gift to us is not an answer to all of our questions. No, his greatest gift to us is way better than a set of answers. God's greatest gift to a man going through the pain of miscarriage is the gift of himself. He carries everything you need into this moment of pain and loss in his loving, wise, and almighty hands. If you are God's child, it is impossible for you to be alone in the dark night of miscarriage, and it's equally impossible for you to be left to your little bag of coping mechanisms. In the gift of himself, God gives you so much more than you could ever stretch your imagination to ask him for. The book you are about to read describes in remarkable detail what it means to know that, in hardship, God gives himself to you. It describes how the glorious truth of God's faithful and loving presence changes how you think about and walk through the dark night of miscarriage.

I can give no higher praise than to say that, with all of its helpful insights and answers, the best thing this book gives you is Jesus. No, not in some super-spiritual, other-worldly way, but in showing us a Jesus who lives with wisdom, power, faithfulness, and grace in the dark cracks and crevasses of human suffering. This is a Jesus who gets what you're going through, and, because he does, offers you just what you need. If you have walked through or are now walking through a miscarriage, I wholeheartedly recommend this book to you. I wish I'd had it when we lost our first child.

Paul David Tripp
December 2021

Introduction

F riend, I wish you and I could sit together. I wish that I could see your face and hear your voice. We could be silent or talk. We could share stories or pray. We could discuss our sorrows, our disappointments, and the questions we've faced as men walking through miscarriage. I'd rather be with you in person than through the pages of this book.

My wife and I have experienced four miscarriages. Each was unique, just like yours. I remember so much confusion over what to do, think, feel, and say. I found no miscarriage resource designed specifically for the father. I had nowhere to turn for answers and shared experience. It wasn't something that men talked much about.

Writing this book, I had mixed feelings. I know that every copy sold will represent one or more miscarriages and countless tears. But I wrote to help you grieve, process, and find hope in Jesus. To that end, I'm glad to spend the next 31 days with you—or however long you need in order to finish reading.

I love the opening of the Gospel of Luke:

> *Many have undertaken to compile a narrative*
> *about the events that have been fulfilled among*
> *us, just as the original eyewitnesses and servants*
> *of the word handed them down to us. So it*
> *also seemed good to me, since I have carefully*
> *investigated everything from the very first, to write*
> *to you in an orderly sequence, most honorable*
> *Theophilus, so that you may know the certainty of*
> *the things about which you have been instructed.*
> — *Luke 1:1-4*

It seems that Theophilus, the recipient of the book, had already been told about Jesus. But he didn't have total certainty. Luke had "carefully investigated everything," even talking to the original eyewitnesses. So he decided to write an orderly account of Jesus' life, death, and resurrection, so that Theophilus might know the certainty of these things. That's my hope for you: certainty about who God is for us, even (or especially!) in our suffering.

I could write you an orderly account of my experience with miscarriage. It might bring a sense of solidarity, but that would not bring certainty. My story is useless to comfort your soul and guarantee a future life in which all sadness is wiped away. The only place to turn to for that kind of certainty is the word of God. The story we need is the story of Jesus.

So, I invite you to read and think with me about the story of Jesus as it is told in the book of Luke. We'll find Jesus to be a powerful and compassionate, faithful and surprising companion in our trials. In Jesus, we have a friend who understands the whole of the human experience, from being a baby in the womb to weeping over a loss. In Christ, we learn how to face temptation, anger, and despair. We'll see what it means to be blessed in his kingdom. We'll discover how he helps us to serve and to be served in our grief.

Each chapter is headed by a Scripture reference which identifies where in Luke we'll be, followed by a question common to men walking through miscarriage, which orients us to the topic of the devotional reading. Like most books, this one is designed to be read from front to back—and one chapter per day, for 31 days. However, don't hesitate to skip around if there are pressing questions you need some help with immediately, or to go more slowly if you need.

I suggest setting aside a certain time each day to read. Start by reading the Scripture passage—reading God's word is the most important part. Pray that God would give you understanding. On days with particularly long passages, I will offer a "focus text" reference. The devotion will focus on these verses. So, if you're pressed for time, you may want to read only those.

Then, with your Bible still open and a pencil in hand, read the chapter. As you read, feel free to highlight portions or to write your thoughts in the margins or a notebook. Stop and think or pray as needed.

At the conclusion of the devotion, you will find some reflection questions. You may wish to write out your responses in the journaling space provided or in a notebook.

It may be helpful to write out your prayers along with your reflections. I encourage you to keep a list of your prayer requests somewhere in the book—at the end of each chapter or inside the cover. I think you'll find encouragement a month from now when you can look back over your thoughts and prayers and see what God has done and is doing.

At the end of the book, you'll find appendices containing some practical help on a variety of topics. They're written by wise and experienced friends. Take advantage of these.

I prayed for you, friend, as I wrote every chapter of this book. I'll pray for you regularly as I see this book on my desk. You're not in this alone. Jesus loves the broken and downcast. He suffered so that he could help us in our suffering. Go into this next month with confidence that God will give you grace.

> *Because of our God's merciful compassion,*
> *the dawn from on high will visit us*
> *to shine on those who live in darkness*
> *and the shadow of death,*
> *to guide our feet into the way of peace.*
>
> — *Luke 1:78-79*

A note on language: throughout the book, I will refer to the mother who miscarried as your "wife." I realize that you may not be married to the mother of your child. In fact, it is possible that she is no longer in your life. Please know that I use the term "wife" for the sake of consistency, not to make you feel sadness or shame. While there may be chapters that offer little application to your circumstances, know that whatever your situation, you're welcome in the pages of this book. Even better, Jesus welcomes you to come to him.

Eric Schumacher

Am I the Only One Who Has Experienced This?

I was a teenager the first time I heard of someone having a miscarriage. I don't recall another mention of it for a decade—not from anyone, and certainly not from a man. I was in seminary the first time I listened to a man share openly about miscarriage.

Miscarriage is common: 10-20 percent of known pregnancies end this way.[1] Talking about miscarriage, especially among men, is much less common. It is a painful and emotionally complicated experience that deals with personal and sometimes private matters. There are multiple reasons why many people choose never to talk about it.

But that can make miscarriage seem incredibly lonely. We may ask if we're the only ones walking through this experience. Do our friends see us? Does God see us?

At the start of Luke, we meet Zechariah and Elizabeth.

---

1 www.mayoclinic.org/diseases-conditions/pregnancy-loss-miscarriage/symptoms-causes/syc-20354298 (accessed Jul. 7 2021).

We learn they could not have children and were beyond the age of childbearing (Luke 1:7). In their culture, couples did not choose to be childless. This means they had been married and trying (and praying) to have children for decades.

It's remarkable, isn't it? A book about Jesus opens with a story about a couple that could not have children. God is well aware of suffering like yours.

In fact, the Bible's storyline includes endless stories about the struggle to have babies. Israel's patriarchs—Abraham, Isaac, and Jacob—were each in (unintentionally) childless marriages. Women of faith such as Ruth and Hannah were childless despite many years of marriage. These years of "barrenness" likely included miscarriage—maybe multiple miscarriages.[2] So these are not just stories of childlessness but of hidden pregnancy loss. Whether you despair of ever

---

2 I posed the question of whether "barrenness" could include miscarriage to Dr. Sandra Glahn. This was her answer (printed here with her permission):

"The word 'barren' comes from an agricultural metaphor. In first-century physiology, the woman had a 'garden,' and it either produced or did not produce. (There was no concept of male infertility or sterility.) A woman might suspect she was pregnant when she missed what seemed to be about the right time for her period or experienced nausea. But until she felt the baby kick, she did not know for sure she was carrying a child. We do not find miscarriage mentioned because the concepts of trimesters and miscarriages probably were not even a thing. For example, all my eight miscarriages happened before the sixth week. Without HCG tests and sonograms, I never would have even known for sure that I was pregnant. Such a woman would be considered barren because there was no child.

"'Barren' meant 'not giving birth.' However you got there, whether via never conceiving or via miscarrying, the reality was the same. No baby = barren. The garden was not flourishing."

having children at all or you are grieving a miscarriage while caring for older kids, the Bible is not unfamiliar with your suffering. You are certainly not alone.

It's common to wonder, "Is this miscarriage the result of something I did wrong, some sin I've committed?" or "Is this a sign that God is angry with me?" The answer is no. Biologically, the majority of miscarriages occur because the baby is not developing correctly. Spiritually, we have no reason to believe that miscarriage indicates God's anger or results from a particular sin. Zechariah and Elizabeth are proof.

Elizabeth spoke of her barrenness as a "disgrace among the people" (v 25). People in their day likely assumed childlessness indicated something shameful. *I wonder what they did to cause God to withhold a child? They must be cursed!* people may have whispered. But not so, Luke tells us! Did you notice verse 6? "Both were righteous in God's sight, living without blame according to all the commands and requirements of the Lord." God saw them as righteous and looked upon them with "favor" (v 25). Their barrenness was not the result of God's displeasure.

After a lifetime of childlessness, Zechariah had a son— and not just any son. John the Baptist would prepare people to meet the Lord (v 17). Likewise, Abraham, Isaac, and Jacob knew many years of undesired childlessness and pregnancy loss—but through their family line, the Messiah arrived. These stories do not just remind us that God sees us in our suffering. They also point to the hope he has provided for us.

Don't mishear me: these stories aren't guarantees that any of us will have a living child one day. They highlight the way that when all human hope is lost, God miraculously delivers his people. The ultimate miracle is Jesus. The message for us in this passage is that our God saves suffering, shamed, and sinful people like you and me.

Zechariah and Elizabeth's son signals the promise of mercy and hope. The angel said of him, "Many will rejoice at his birth" (v 14). John the Baptist would announce the arrival of Jesus, our Savior. It is through him that Elizabeth's words can become our own—*the Lord has looked on us with favor and taken away our disgrace!* May we, like Elizabeth and Mary (and, eventually, Zechariah), receive this good news in faith.

Friend, God sees your suffering. He's provided mercy and hope through Jesus. Through the Holy Spirit, God walks with us through this darkness. Let's ask him to provide much comfort as we journey through the Gospel of Luke these next thirty days.

———

Father, you know my sorrow. You know every hurt of my heart. Be merciful to me in this suffering. Show me who Jesus is. Help me to trust in him to lead me through the valley of the shadow of death to the green pastures of life. Amen.

REFLECT

- What do you have in common with Zechariah and Elizabeth?
- How many reasons for hope can you see in what you've read?

JOURNAL

2. LUKE 1:26-80

Have I Really Lost a Child?

"My bones were not hidden from you when I was made in secret," David says to the Lord (Psalm 139:15). Secret. Unseen by anyone but the Lord. Until the last century, no one had ever seen what was happening in the womb as the Lord formed our bodies. Even now, with modern technology, most of pregnancy is out of sight. Miscarriage is, by nature, an unseen thing.

Parents often do not see their miscarried child, particularly if the miscarriage has happened in the early stages of pregnancy. Of our four miscarried pregnancies, we only saw the body of one baby. The child was so small it fit in the palm of my hand. As we marveled at the tiny bones—fingers, toes, ribs—we knew this was a child, a person. But without such an opportunity, parents may experience uncertainty.

"If a tree falls in the woods and no one is there to hear it, does it still make a sound?" That proverbial riddle ultimately asks, *If a human being has not witnessed a thing, did it really exist?* For a father in miscarriage, it becomes, *If no one saw or held what was developing in my wife's womb, was it really a child? Can something so small (or undeveloped or hidden or dependent or...) really be a human being?*

The question matters for many reasons.[3] For miscarrying parents, the answer shapes how we understand our mourning. *If this was not a child, are we merely mourning the loss of potential?* The question over the fetus's status is muddled by a culture that does not value life in the womb. Family, friends, or co-workers may make stinging remarks. "Well, at least you didn't lose a child!" Such circumstances challenge the legitimacy of our grief. Who mourns a lump of cells? I certainly don't lament over a pulled tooth.

Fortunately, today's passage provides a clear and helpful answer. What begins to grow at conception is a human being—as human as you and me.

The angel says to Mary, "You will conceive and give birth to a son." She will do two things—conceive and give birth. But those actions have only one object: "a son." What she conceives and what she gives birth to is the same thing—a human child.

Luke tells us that the "baby leaped for joy" inside Elizabeth (Luke 1:41, 44). That word "baby" is the same in Luke 2:16—"They hurried off and found both Mary and Joseph, and the baby who was lying in the manger." What leaped in Elizabeth's womb is the same type of thing as what the shepherds found swaddled in a manger—a human baby.

---

3 For example, the SLED test developed by Stand to Reason demonstrates that Size, Level of Development, Environment, and Dependency have no bearing on the value of a human life. This may be helpful to review as an assurance of the value of your baby's brief life (see www.str.org/w/the-sled-test).

Through these clear statements in God's word, the Holy Spirit shows us how God views what starts growing at conception. In God's sight, this is a child, a baby. Who are we to disagree with the author of life?

This has implications for you too, friend. If what you lost is a baby, it implies you are a father. No matter its size, level of development, environment, or dependency on its mother—this was your baby. Even if no one saw or held this baby, you are a father. So, you have every reason to mourn: you are a father who lost your child.

Feel free to pause and let that sink in. It's ok to weep, to mourn, to grieve. You wouldn't shame a father for crying over the death of his two-year-old. So, you should feel no shame in grieving your loss. You are experiencing death.

Zechariah speaks of those "who live in darkness and the shadow of death" (v 79). Though he is speaking of more than pregnancy loss, his words certainly capture how miscarriage can feel. These are dark days. You may feel like you're walking in the shadowlands. The world seems dim and unclear. But there is good news for us here. Dwelling in darkness prepares us to appreciate the light.

Before we go on, I invite you to reread Mary's and Zechariah's words (v 46-55, 68-79). Mark the words of hope expressed over the birth of Jesus and that of John, who announces him.

Mary praises the Lord because he sees "the humble condition of his servant" and extends mercy (v 48, 50). The Lord sees your humble condition, friend. He has gracious favor for us. Such hope is based on what the

Lord does for us (v 49) and not on what our bodies can do for him.

Who receives this mercy from the Lord? It is for "those who fear him" (v 50). God's mercy comes to those who trust in him, not to those who trust in their failing flesh.

God really is the helper of his people (v 54). Who does a helper help? Not the one who is healthy and full! A helper assists the one who needs help—the one who is weak and empty. The Lord has always been a God who sees his people's misery and responds with compassion (v 54-55).

This is good news indeed! Through Jesus, God "has visited and provided redemption for his people" (v 68). Through Jesus' life, death, and resurrection, God brings us salvation through the forgiveness of our sins (v 77). In Christ, God's merciful compassion visits and shines on us in the shadow of death, guiding our feet to peace (v 78-79).

Perhaps you've found it difficult to pray in your grief. Maybe you don't know what to pray. Take a moment now to read aloud Mary's and Zechariah's words (v 46-55, 68-79). Make them your prayer. May God hear and give us the grace to believe and be comforted.

REFLECT

- Have you registered that you are a father? How do you feel about that?
- What phrase from what you've read is the most helpful for you right now?

JOURNAL

How Do I Deal with So Much Uncertainty?

One day you were planning the perfect nursery. The next day you learned the baby would never sleep in it. Yesterday you were designing a baby announcement. Today you're trying to decide how to tell your family the hard news.

Things that once seemed certain are gone, and so much uncertainty remains. *Will my wife be ok? Will we be able to get pregnant again? Will we have another miscarriage? What if we never have a living child?*

When you think of the Christmas story in Luke 2, I wonder what ideas come to mind. Warm tones? Cozy surroundings? A calm and silent night? Look again. Do you see the reasons for fear and uncertainty in the opening paragraph?

There had never been a registration of this kind (v 1-2). *What was Caesar up to? What did this mean for the future of the Jewish people?*

Joseph and Mary had to take a grueling 90-mile trip

from Nazareth to Bethlehem (v 4-5). Imagine taking a physically demanding five-day trip with a wife who is heavily pregnant. *Will she be ok? What if she goes into labor in the middle of nowhere? Will we find lodging? Will we encounter thieves or wild animals?*

Then, arriving, there is no guest room available, even as Mary goes into labor (v 6-7). It's possible, given the scandal of their unwed pregnancy, that their family had shunned them—so instead they had to lodge with animals. Mary had never given birth before, and this birth would not occur in a sterilized labor and delivery room. There would be no modern medicine to prevent infection. Imagine the anxious thoughts and concerns that must have weighed on Joseph's mind.

God sometimes calls his people to (and puts them in) frightening and uncertain circumstances. He has never given his people *every* detail ahead of time. But he *has* given us good reason not to be afraid.

In the next scene, the angel of the Lord stood before the shepherds (v 9). "The glory of the Lord shone around them." How terrifying would that be? But the angel told them not to be afraid because he had brought good news: "Today in the city of David a Savior was born for you, who is the Messiah, the Lord" (v 11).

Uncertainty creates fear because we can't control the outcome. Miscarriage presses this point home like nothing else. I felt so weak and helpless, unable to do anything to guarantee the baby's safety in my wife's womb. Neither the doctors nor I could stop death. After my wife delivered our dead baby, I watched her bleed. The nurses rushed her to surgery. All I could do was sit in our room, alone, and pray. I did not control the outcome.

Death entered the world through sin (Romans 5:12). Until sin is gone, death is our only certainty. But sin *will* be gone.

Your child was not born alive. But a Savior *was* born to you.

Don't move past that word too quickly. Jesus is a Savior. He came to obliterate sin and death through his death and resurrection. Eternal life is now our certainty if we trust in him.

This Savior is the Messiah. That means he is God's anointed King. He is the Lord. That means he is God. Our Savior is the King who is God. That means he reigns. Period. No debate. It is settled. Jesus is the sovereign over all things. It is inevitable: his will shall come to pass.

What is God's will for us? "Peace on earth to people he favors!" (Luke 2:14). If you trust in Jesus, then you're among those people. Peace is yours—and that's *certain*.

———

One day, there will be peace on earth. Jesus will raise us from the dead to live and reign with him. But, until then, we live in a world of hardship. As Joseph and Mary presented their son to the Lord, they met a prophet, Simeon. He had an unsettling message for Mary: "A sword will pierce your own soul" (v 35).

How do you think that landed on Joseph? *What does that mean? What's going to happen to her? What can I do?* You may be asking similar questions right now.

Indeed, a sword would pierce Mary's soul. She would watch Roman soldiers mock, spit on, beat, and execute her firstborn son. God's blessing and promise of peace did not mean a comfortable life for her—nor for us.

But even in our loss and discomfort, we have another assurance. God continues to bless and use his people. We see that when we look at Anna (v 36-38).

Anna had been a widow for 84 years. We can assume those years weren't carefree. Her arms were empty—no husband, no children. But she had the Lord.

Anna lived out her years in God's house, serving him with fasting and prayers. Mary told us that the Lord satisfies the hungry with good things (1:53), and he certainly had a good thing for Anna. Her emptiness and disappointment were the place where God allowed her to serve. She would see the newborn Messiah—and be the first to declare his arrival in the temple (2:38).

Do you have a friend who has also gone through a miscarriage? Answering your questions, offering wisdom, and providing solidarity may be a way God calls him to serve from his emptiness. Would you be willing to share your loss with him and ask if he might walk with you? If you don't know of such a person, ask your pastor. He likely knows of someone.

And as you journey through miscarriage, consider keeping a little journal. Write down the questions and concerns you have, and what you wish someone had told you or done for you. Keep this on hand for future opportunities to serve a friend walking through loss.

The Jesus born in fearful and uncertain circumstances is now the exalted King. He looks on you with love. He promises you peace. What's more, he is using you even now.

REFLECT

- What feels uncertain right now? What is certain?
- How might God use you to bless others, even at this time?

JOURNAL

What Is Jesus Doing?

Last Christmas, my daughter gave me a hamster. Cash (named after Johnny) lives in a habitat on my desk. The first day, he let me reach in and pick him up. I thought we were growing close to each other. Then he started to nip at my fingers. Then he bit me—hard.

I still hold him and pet him. Once he's in my hand, he's fine. But I'm much more cautious in approaching him now. I'm not so sure I can trust him.

Have you had such an experience with a person you love and trust? You thought you knew them. Then, without any explanation, they did something you never expected. Perhaps they hurt you. It makes trust difficult.

Miscarriage is like that for many people. I've counseled many parents who say, "I don't understand what God is doing! Why would God bring me this pain? Why would he treat me this way? This makes it really hard for me to trust him." Have you said the same? If so, you're not the first, and you won't be the last.

Joseph and Mary asked a similar question of Jesus: "Son, why have you treated us like this?" (Luke 2:48). They'd been in Jerusalem for the Passover and were returning home. They may have believed that Jesus was playing with his cousins. Or Joseph assumed Mary was watching him, and Mary thought Joseph had him. Whatever the reason for the oversight, after a full day of travel, they realized that Jesus was not with them. Not finding him in the traveling party, the couple turned around and headed back to Jerusalem.

Can you imagine the conversation Joseph and Mary had on the way? *"I thought you had him!" "Me?! He always travels with you! Why didn't you say anything?"* And then silence. After a full day of travel to get back to the city, they searched there for *three* days.

My son got lost at the zoo once. It probably took us 30 minutes to find him safely reading a book at the security station. But it seemed like an eternity as I retraced our steps and looked in each bathroom stall! Every missing-person drama I'd viewed raced through my head. I imagined the worst. I scolded myself. Panic, sadness, anger, guilt, regret, and confusion coursed through my body.

My heart *hurt* after just 30 minutes. What must have Joseph and Mary felt after three days?

At last, they found their twelve-year-old son sitting among the teachers in the temple. Astonished, Mary asked him, "Son, why have you treated us like this? Your father and I have been anxiously searching for you" (v 48).

Notice what Mary's question implies. She's saying that

Jesus did something to them. He treated them a certain way, and it resulted in trauma. He hurt them. *I trusted you, Jesus. How could you treat us this way?* That may be what you, too, are saying right now.

Does it seem strange to you to say that Jesus hurt you? Acknowledgment of hurt is not necessarily an accusation of wrongdoing. Doctors may cause hurt while treating us for our good. It's ok to acknowledge that God brings us pain. Job did just that—and he didn't sin in doing so (Job 1:20-22). Jesus did the same on the cross (Matthew 27:46).

Jesus gave his parents an answer that is good for us to hear. "Didn't you know that it was necessary for me to be in my Father's house?" (Luke 2:49). That answer must have stung a bit. *You're the adults. I'm the twelve-year-old here. If I get this, why don't you?* Besides, they're not the ultimate parents in Jesus' equation—God is. Jesus must carry out his Father's will, not theirs. Ouch.

Jesus had to be attentive to his Father—in his house, listening to his Father's word, doing what the Father had for him to do. That necessity didn't end when Jesus entered adulthood. Throughout his life, Jesus could only do what he saw the Father doing (John 5:19). That is good news for a few reasons. It means Jesus succeeded where we fail. He obeyed where we have not. And when we put our faith in him, this perfect record is counted as if it were ours, too (Philippians 3:9).

It is also good news because Jesus is still devoted to doing his Father's will by bringing his mission to completion.

What is the Father's will? Jesus said, "This is the will of him who sent me: that I should lose none of those he has given me but should raise them up on the last day" (John 6:39).

Right now, Jesus is devoted to not losing you. Even amid this terrible pain, Jesus is entirely dedicated to you and your good. He is still in prayer in his Father's house—and his prayers are for you (Hebrews 7:25). He is the one who keeps you going every day, and he is the one who *will* raise you on the final day. He will raise you from the dead and wipe every tear from your eye. "Death will be no more; grief, crying, and pain will be no more" (Revelation 21:4).

I love how our passage ends. Mary and Joseph were still clueless about what had just happened (Luke 2:50). They must have had so many questions. *What on earth did he mean? Why did he do that?* Even though we know that Jesus loves us and is devoted to our good, his word can still leave us scratching our heads.

So, don't cast this hurt out of your mind and seek to forget it. Instead, be like Mary, who "kept all these things in her heart" (v 51). Treasure the fact that Jesus is doing his Father's will, even though that might still seem confusing and painful. Delight in the fact that he knows what he's doing—and what he's doing is loving and saving you.

REFLECT

- What questions are you asking of God at the moment?
- What does Jesus' devotion to you mean for you today?

JOURNAL

5. LUKE 3:1-20

What Does It Look Like to Honor Jesus in This?

I've never been good at handling stress, uncertainty, and sorrow. The natural responses of my flesh are sinful and damaging. I lash out with my words, harming my wife and children. I turn to food for a moment's satisfaction—and then I turn to it again, and again, and again. I sleep too much, escaping into unconsciousness so that I don't have to deal with life. I distract myself with Netflix, social media, or games on my phone. I withdraw into myself, withholding my thoughts, words, and affection from my friends and family. I "fake it 'til I make it," putting on a good face and acting as though everything is ok. But on the inside, I tear myself up with self-hatred, despair, and guilt.

I know. I'm a pastor. I'm supposed to have it all together as the perfect model of Christ-likeness. Guess what. I don't.

Miscarriage brings tension, sadness, and confusion all at once. Our sinful nature and Satan see their chance and pounce. Many men respond in the ways I've described above. That leaves us asking: How do I fight sin when I'm stressed? How do I maintain a good witness with my family, neighbors, and church? What does it look like to honor Jesus in this?

Or, "What then should we do?" That's the question the people asked John the Baptist as he preached a message of repentance (Luke 3:10). Repentance means a change of thinking, behaving, and feeling concerning our sin. Repentance from sin accompanies genuine faith in Jesus. When we experience forgiveness, we want to leave sin and live in a new way (v 3, 7-9).

There are many ways to cope with stress, uncertainty, and grief. It's worth seeking out practical insights on healthy coping strategies. But for now, let's think specifically about our sinful responses. What does it mean to repent?

John encourages the crowds to practice compassion (v 11). He tells tax collectors to be honest and not steal (v 13). He says soldiers must not abuse their power for the sake of gain at another's loss (v 14).

Compassion, honesty, and acting justly toward one's neighbor. How do these calls to repentance apply to fathers walking through miscarriage?

Each of these commands teaches us to love our neighbor as ourselves. Jesus said this is the second greatest command in the law (Matthew 22:39). So, we might start by asking this question: if my neighbor suffered a stressful and sudden loss, how would I want him to treat me? I wouldn't want him to abuse me with his words or his fists. I wouldn't want him to withdraw from our relationship, grow bitter because I've failed him, or pretend that all is ok when it is not. I wouldn't want him to dive into destructive ways of coping. I would like him to be honest with me, so I would know how to help and pray. Perhaps honoring Christ in miscarriage means being open and gentle with our neighbors. "Neighbor" includes our wife, other children, friends, church family, co-workers, and medical staff.

Has such love described you so far? If you're like me, it probably doesn't—at least not entirely. So what should we do?

First, admit the sin. There's no use trying to hide it or spin it. God sees it. Chances are, our wife and friends do too. John the Baptist didn't call people to cover up sin or deny it. The first step in repenting is admitting we've sinned.

Admit the sin to God. Ask him to forgive you and to help you change. Next, admit the sin to those you've sinned against. Name it, don't excuse it—and ask for forgiveness. "Honey, I lashed out at you with angry words. I know they hurt you. That was sinful on my part. I love you and don't want to treat you like that. Will you forgive me?" Depending on the nature of the hurt, it may take some time for forgiveness to come. That's ok. Your part is to ask for forgiveness and change your behavior. You can't change your neighbor.

Finally, confess to a trusted friend or pastor. God does not intend for us to fight sin alone. "Pastor, ever since the miscarriage, I haven't known how to deal with it. I'm pretending everything is ok, but I'm a mess on the inside. Could you help me stop this and follow Jesus?"

Having confessed your sin, look for ways to love your neighbor. Your wife and kids (if you have others) are suffering too. Consider ways to minister to them in their grief. Look for ways to turn to and serve Jesus together.

Perhaps it would be good to stop now and examine where you can practice the repentance that John described. These may be helpful questions:

- How do I have more than I need (Luke 3:11)—time, strength, wealth, etc.? How could I share those things with my family?
- In what ways am I tempted to demand too much (v 13)? How might I ask too much of my wife or my children?
- In what ways might I be tempted to sin against others because of lack of contentment with my circumstances (v 14)—envy, bitterness, anger?

John didn't only preach repentance; "he proclaimed the good news to the people" (v 18). The good news was that Jesus was coming to bring God's kingdom. The coming King would remove sin, destroy death, trample the devil, and set his people free. Jesus would baptize his people with the Holy Spirit (v 16). John could only call people to repent, but Jesus would make them holy.

God won't give us the silent treatment when we bring him our sin. Bringing sinners out of sin is what Jesus wants to do! So, he not only forgives us; he gives us his Holy Spirit to help us change. That means we need not be afraid to confess our sins and repent. The Lord is present and ready to help us in our need.

REFLECT

- What's hard about repentance?
- What did the people John was addressing hope for? What hope is there here for you?

JOURNAL

Does God Know What I'm Going Through?

We spent time in a hospital during our third miscarriage. When they admitted my wife, they put an identification band on her wrist. I did not receive one. Only patients got the bands—mothers, living babies, and the fathers of *living* children. That meant that I couldn't leave and re-enter easily. I was stopped at the nurses' station—and then had to explain that "Yes, I am a father" and "No, I don't have a band" and then "I don't have a band because our baby died." I felt excluded and forgotten. It was as though, now that my baby had been miscarried, the nurses didn't see me or care whether I existed.

Do you ever wonder that about your Creator, the one who dwells in heaven and rules over all things? Does he think of you? Does he know about your miscarriage? Does he see and care about your suffering? Keep reading; our passage addresses those questions.

The genealogies in the Bible may strike us as a bit boring. Why does Luke include this long list of names after Jesus' baptism? And why was *Jesus* baptized? (And what does any of this have to do with miscarriage?!)

At Jesus' baptism, his Father made an announcement unlike any other. As Jesus prayed, the heavens split open. The Holy Spirit descended on him. Then God the Father spoke from heaven: "You are my beloved Son; with you I am well-pleased" (Luke 3:22).

That's the main point that Luke wants to make: Jesus is the Son of God. That's one reason he includes the genealogy (v 23-38). Strangely, Luke traces Jesus' lineage through his adoptive father, Joseph, to prove that he is the Son of God.

You may have found it challenging to pay attention as you read this genealogy. After all, there are so many names of men about whom we know nothing! But isn't that a comforting thought? All these fathers may be forgotten to history, but God never forgot them. They lived real lives, and God knew them. He remembers their names. And this gives us hope that God really does see and know each one of us in our suffering.

———

God is a parent; he has children. Luke calls Adam, God's direct creation, the "son of God" (v 38). In some sense, we all descend from God. He is our Maker, our "first Father." But Luke's genealogy demonstrates that Jesus has a special line of descent. It's significant that he's descended from Adam, Abraham, and David—special men to whom God revealed parts of his plan of salvation. By being born into this family, Jesus is both the recipient and fulfillment of all God's saving promises.

God knew that sin and death would be passed along to Adam's descendants, including us. Out of love for us, God announced to Adam his plan of salvation. He promised the birth of a child who would strike the serpent's head (Genesis 3:15). This long list of names reminds us that—from generation to generation—God did not forget his promise. The story has many twists and turns, but Jesus was always going to be there at the end: God born as man, for the sake of each one of us.

———

Of course, we already know that Jesus is the Son of God. We learned that with the angel's announcement to Mary. While it's important that Jesus is descended from Adam, Abraham, David, and the rest, it's even more important that he is the unique, unparalleled, one-of-a-kind Son of God. We, as God's creatures, "all have sinned and fall short of the glory of God" (Romans 3:23). Not so with this Son of God—Jesus is an especially loved Son, one that makes his Father very happy (Luke 3:22). Unlike us, the Son of God is without sin, entirely pleasing to his Father (Hebrews 4:15).

So then why was Jesus baptized? Didn't we read that John preached "a baptism of repentance for the forgiveness of sins" (Luke 3:3)? Why would a sinless man receive a baptism of repentance? He had no sins to forgive!

It wasn't enough for Jesus merely to be born human. He had to come to live as our substitute. So, in his baptism,

Jesus identified with us, the sinners he came to save. Though he did not need to repent, he willingly identified with repenters. Later, he would take the place of sinners in his death, even though he had no sin. That is one of many reasons that the Father announced his pleasure in his Son. The Son was doing what the Father sent him to do.

———

Generation after generation, God was working to bring salvation to his people. To Abraham, he promised an uncountable number of descendants—and you are one of them! To David, he promised a Son with an eternal kingdom—and you are one of his citizens! He's always known us; he's never forgotten us. That includes our sufferings. Our Father has recorded our sufferings in his book and collected our tears in a bottle (Psalm 56:8).

In the end, Jesus' identification with us would mean his death under the wrath of God. Think of it: God had a Son he loved, a Son who gave him incredible pleasure. That Son died. Think of it: God knows what it is to experience the death of a child. That means that he can identify with you in your suffering.

We can take comfort in all this. God understands what we are suffering. He's watched his Son die. He's been keeping track of our sufferings so that he can comfort us in each one. More than that, Jesus identified with us in our grief and sin so that we would join him in his eternal life.

If Jesus identified with our sufferings, we can be confident that he sees them now. If Jesus died to save us, we can be sure that he won't desert us now. Jesus became human, lived, died, and rose to save you, friend. Rest in knowing he loves you and is with you always.

REFLECT

- Has anything made you think that God has forgotten or ignored you?
- Do you think much about how Jesus is a son, a child? Does it change the way you see him?

JOURNAL

How Do I Fight the Temptation to Despair?

When we experienced our first miscarriage, we grieved. But we were not so concerned about having more children. We'd had three successful pregnancies and now a miscarriage. One in four pregnancies miscarry. So, painful as the miscarriage was, we were able to comfort ourselves with the thought that, statistically, this was normal.

But years later, when we were longing to have more children, we had our third miscarriage. At that point, doubts crept in. *What if we can't have another child? What if we have another miscarriage?*

Miscarriage can challenge our faith—and not just our hope about childbearing. It challenges our hope in God, tempting us to despair of God's goodness, faithfulness, and provision. Is God withholding what we need to be happy?

Our flesh is frail. Sin lives in us. What we want to do, we don't. What we don't want to do, we do (Romans 7:14-25).

We want to trust God, but we fail. We don't want to despair, but we do.

It doesn't help that we have an enemy in Satan. He's a ruthless enemy. He doesn't back off when he sees injury. No, when he smells blood, he attacks. Miscarriage is a prime opportunity for this wicked lion to pounce on us. So what are we to do?

In the first place, if you have already given yourself over to despair, stop here and pray. Tell God what you're thinking, how you're feeling. Ask him to help you. He's a good Father, who loves to help us.

In the previous chapter, we considered how Jesus came to identify with us in every way, but without sin. In today's reading, we begin to see what this looks like—and what it means for us.

Jesus emerged from the baptismal waters to go into a barren, inhospitable place. He would be there for 40 days, tempted by the devil. He ate nothing during those 40 days—and, in case we missed the point, Luke adds, "He was hungry" (Luke 4:2).

The devil struck when Jesus was weak and deprived. He challenged Jesus to prove that he was God's beloved Son. Instead of trusting God, he should use his power to serve himself and make bread from stones (v 3). Instead of obeying God's call to die to save the nations, he should strike a deal with the devil and worship Satan in exchange for the kingdoms of the world (v 5-6). Instead of believing that God would raise him from the dead when the time came, he should test God's care (v 9-11).

Stop a moment and reflect on your temptations. Does Jesus' experience in any way connect with yours? Are you tempted to turn to earthly comforts and forget about God? Do you engage in risky behavior to distract yourself from the pain, putting the Lord's protection to the test? Or maybe you're looking to modern idols for provision instead of God.

Take a moment, once again, to pray. Make your specific temptations known to God. Ask him to carry them for you, believing that he cares about you (1 Peter 5:7).

Jesus did not succumb to Satan's temptations. Instead, he believed God's word. He countered each temptation with truth from Scripture. Jesus trusted his Father and obeyed his word. He faced the devil, and he won.

The wilderness temptation of Jesus offers us hope in several ways. First, it reminds us that Jesus wins—and we win in him! Remember that Jesus is our substitute. He succeeded in resisting temptation where we fail. He also bore the consequences of our failings on the cross. When we trust in Christ, God sees his obedience as our obedience and his death as our death. That means that, though we fail, God does not condemn us (Romans 8:1). We can fight temptation by believing that Jesus has already won for us.

Jesus also serves as an example of how God's children should live. He fought temptation, even in painful hunger, by trusting in God's word. Christ treasured God's word in his heart so that he would not sin (Psalm 119:11). The Spirit is with us, as he was with Jesus.

Through his help, we begin to treasure God's word as we study it. The Spirit will help us remember and believe in times of trouble.

So, if you are tempted to despair, read God's word. The Psalms especially are a wonderful resource, giving us words for our feelings of despair, doubt, and hopelessness. Try praying aloud a lament, such as Psalm 22, 25, 42, 77, or 88. Or look at Isaiah 53, a prophetic description of Jesus and his suffering. Consider an account of Jesus voicing his own grief, such as Matthew 27:46 or Mark 14:32-42. Or meditate on Paul's thoughts on perseverance in hardship (see 2 Corinthians 4 or Romans 8:12-39). Read any of these passages aloud; let the words of Scripture become your own in prayer to God.

After all, the story of Jesus' temptation should also encourage us to pray. Jesus "has been tempted in every way as we are" so that he can "sympathize with our weaknesses" (Hebrews 4:15). That means we should keep the faith and go with boldness to God in prayer, where we find help when we need it (Hebrews 4:16). "For since he himself has suffered when he was tempted, he is able to help those who are tempted" (Hebrews 2:18).

Stop now and pray again. Thank God for giving you his Son, his Spirit, and his word. Ask God to help you remember Jesus' victory every day, especially in temptation. Ask him to help you treasure his word so that you don't sin. Ask him to lift your eyes in hope and not despair.

REFLECT

- What tempts you to despair?
- What habits of prayer and Bible reading would you like to cultivate?

JOURNAL

8. LUKE 5

(Focus verses: 1-32)

Am I Too Sinful
for Jesus to Love?

In Jesus' day, some people believed that suffering was a punishment from God for those who had been particularly sinful (see Luke 13:1-5). Even though Jesus rejected this idea, it persists today. You may be tempted to believe miscarriage is a punishment for sin. Someone suggested to my friend that she miscarried because she failed to pray enough.

I worried that our baby died because of some sinful thing I'd done. If only I had sinned less, we'd still have the baby. Other times I'd start believing that it happened because I hadn't done enough good. If I had spent more time reading the Bible, then this baby would be alive. Either way, the devil would suggest that the baby died because I didn't measure up. This miscarriage was my fault.

Are you tempted to think this way? Do you wonder if you might be too sinful for Jesus to love? If so, take a few minutes to consider the merciful Lord we meet in Luke 5:1-32. Here, we find the compassionate heart of Jesus on full display. We see a Savior who comforts, cleanses, forgives, befriends, and calls sinners. No one—not you, not me—is too sinful for Jesus to love.

Jesus comforts sinners (v 1-11). When Peter saw the miraculous catch of fish that Jesus provided, he knew that Jesus was Lord. Peter also knew that he had no business being in the Lord's presence. He was too sinful. So he cried out, "Go away from me, because I'm a sinful man, Lord!" But Jesus would not leave. Instead, he comforted Peter—"Don't be afraid" (v 8-10). If you feel too sinful to be with Jesus, this is also his word to you. "Don't be afraid." The Jesus we're about to see is a man of good news for sinful people.

Jesus cleanses sinners (v 12-16). Like Peter, the man with leprosy knew that he was unclean. He did not have leprosy because of any particular sin, but the Law of Moses declared him to be unclean—a physical illustration of sin—and forbade him from entering the Lord's presence. He had to live outside the city and announce his uncleanness to everyone (Leviticus 13:45-46). But unlike Peter, this man knew that Jesus could change him. So he fell on his face and begged Jesus to make him clean. Jesus touched him, and the leprosy was gone. That, we will see, is why Jesus came—to make unclean people fit for his presence.

Jesus forgives sinners (v 17-26). This is a fantastic story. Four friends had faith that Jesus could heal their paralyzed friend. So they dropped in on a teaching session. Literally. They carried their friend to the crowded house where Jesus was teaching. Unable to enter the house, they carried him up to the flat roof. They removed the tiles and lowered their friend right down in front of Jesus!

Everyone expected Jesus to heal the man's paralysis. Instead, seeing their faith, Jesus said, "Friend, your sins are forgiven" (v 20). Then he proved his authority by healing the man.

That's some good news. Jesus didn't forgive the man because he deserved it. No, Jesus forgave his sins on the basis of *faith*. God forgives by grace through our faith and not based on our works (Ephesians 2:8-9).

Jesus befriends sinners (v 27-32). The Jews hated the Romans, who had taken over their land and ruled over them. That is why they despised Jewish tax collectors. These brothers betrayed Israel to serve Rome—and collected extra for themselves!

So imagine the shock when Jesus walked up to a tax collector's office and told the man, Levi, to follow him. Levi accepted Jesus' invitation. He invited Jesus, his disciples, and many of his own tax collector friends to join him.

The religious leaders threw a fit. *Why on earth would Jesus and his disciples eat and drink with tax collectors and sinners?* they demanded. Jesus, who claimed to be the Son of God, dined with sinners as though he were their friend (see also Matthew 11:19; Luke 15:2, 19:7). They couldn't make sense of it. But that's what Jesus came to do—to make sinners his friends (John 15:15).

Jesus replied to the Pharisees' question, "It is not those who are healthy who need a doctor, but those who are sick. I have not come to call the righteous, but sinners to repentance" (Luke 5:31-32). Jesus' fellowship with sinners was intentional! He was a doctor sent to heal. That meant he had to be around the sick. Jesus was a Savior sent to forgive and change sinners. That meant he had to be with sinners to call them to leave their sin.

Friend, don't believe the lie that your sin makes you unlovable to Jesus. Please don't think that he is punishing you because you're not good enough for him. Jesus is a friend to sinners.

How beautiful is Jesus' love for sinners! He calls us to leave our sin to follow him and receive his gracious forgiveness. He longs to cleanse us with his touch and comfort us with his presence. He offers to make us his friends. All this he gives without cost to those who trust him. And then, as with Peter and Levi, he invites us to join him in his mission.

Do you believe this? Spend time in prayer, thanking God for what we've seen. Ask Jesus to comfort you, cleanse you, forgive you, and assure you of his friendship.

REFLECT

- What is Jesus like, in what you have read here?
- If he were with you physically, how would he respond to you today?

JOURNAL

Is It Ok for Me to Take Time off Work?

In caring for church members in miscarriage, I've seen various responses from employers. Some immediately offer ample time off with encouragement to care for their wife. I also know men who have heard, "This is common. It happens all the time. Time off isn't needed."

Is it reasonable to take time off work to mourn and be with your wife and family? That question might surprise some, as the answer seems obvious to them. But for many men, there are things that make this a stressful decision. What a father should do about his work schedule is an often-overlooked aspect of miscarriage. Each person must make their own decisions, which will vary by situation.

Though it is changing, many American workplaces still do not provide paternity leave. When a man's partner has a baby, he either uses vacation time or goes to work. Elsewhere, paternity leave is a statutory right— but taking time off for a baby that is not alive? That may feel unreasonable—especially in a culture that undervalues life in the womb.

Some church cultures teach and emphasize a deficient understanding of masculine strength. Men become afraid to show any sign of weakness. Time off to mourn the loss of a child he didn't know? Weak! A need for rest? Lazy! Cultural pressures lead some men to neglect their wives in a time of pain.

On the other hand, a financial situation or employment arrangement may require a man to go to work. Such a decision is responsible stewardship and an act of caring for his wife. Or the mother may wish to have as much normality as possible as she processes what's happened. Again, if that's the case—and if you can bear that sense of normality yourself—it may be an act of kindness for you to keep going to work.

In today's reading, the religious leaders took issue with Jesus' Sabbath activities. The law commanded that Israelites observe the seventh day of the week as a Sabbath, a day of rest. The Sabbath reminded the Israelites that God had given them rest in their salvation. It was a gracious gift; unlike the nations that did not know the Lord, they could rest in his provision. The Lord cared about his people and provided them with rest that others could not understand.

Ironically, Israel's leaders themselves failed to understand the point of the Sabbath. They turned the day of rest into an unbending, merciless list of strict rules. They did not understand that there are legitimate exceptions (Luke 6:4). Nor did they recognize that Jesus has the authority to grant such exceptions (v 5).

On one occasion, Jesus found himself teaching in the synagogue on the Sabbath. The religious leaders knew that a man with a shriveled hand was there. They considered healing to be work. So, if Jesus healed this man, they could charge him with breaking the Sabbath and condemn him.

Jesus knew what was happening. So, he brought the man up in front of everyone. Then he posed an insightful and critical question: "Is it lawful to do good on the Sabbath or to do evil, to save life or to destroy it?" (v 9). They had no answer. It is *always* lawful to do good.

How does this help us think about time off after a miscarriage? Time off is by no means a one-to-one parallel with the Sabbath day. But Jesus' rhetorical question is instructive and relevant. It reminds us that there is no hard-and-fast rule about time off. Every miscarriage and circumstance is unique. Deciding what to do is a matter of wisdom, not law.

It is lawful to do good, particularly to a suffering neighbor. Underpinning God's law is the command to love your neighbor as yourself (Matthew 22:38). It's a principle we return to when we seek to know how to live. So, the question we should ask is "Would it be loving for me to take time off to care for my family and to mourn this loss?" If the answer is yes, you should take time off guilt-free. If the answer is no, then you should go to work guilt-free.

Friend, one of the primary ways we show our love for God is by loving those made in his image—our neighbors. Your wife is your closest neighbor and, after God, your priority. God calls you to follow Christ's example. You are to be the first to sacrifice for her good and your unity with her (Ephesians 5:22-31).

Loving your wife and family may come with a cost. Your coworkers or employer might think you're making too big a deal of this. They may look at you as weak or lazy. Perhaps time off will be without pay or counted against you when it comes time for promotions or bonuses. But the Sabbath reminds us that we have a God who works for us, provides for us. Today's reading shows us that Jesus loves his people and doesn't care what others might think of him for it.

In critical moments, Jesus was not afraid to step away and spend time in prayer (Luke 6:12). He didn't care if this upset the expectations of others; he'd come to obey God (4:42-44). So stop now and pray. Ask the Lord to free you from the fear of people and fill you with love for your neighbor. Seek wisdom to know how best to care for your wife, family, and self. Ask for faith to trust God to provide as you obey him. Ask your wife what she needs and how you can best serve her. Listen and seek to understand. Don't worry what others might think. Love her and obey God.

REFLECT

- How did Jesus decide whether to work or rest?
- What helps you (and your wife) to rest well?

JOURNAL

10. LUKE 6:17-26

Why Won't Jesus Bless Us?

I often hear Psalm 127 quoted to celebrate the gift of children:

> Children are a heritage from the LORD,
>   offspring a reward from him.
> Like arrows in the hands of a warrior
>   are children born in one's youth.
> Blessed is the man
>   whose quiver is full of them. — v 3-5 (NIV)

This passage may be found in baby announcements and baby-shower devotions, on Mother's Day and Father's Day, at infant baptisms and baby dedications. These words are Scripture. So they are, of course, good, trustworthy, and profitable. But in our broken world with broken bodies, they can be painful to hear. When poorly translated or inappropriately applied, they can create a crisis of faith.

As miscarriage after miscarriage comes, these words torment the soul. If children are a reward from the Lord, what have I done wrong? What do I need to do to earn this blessing? If a blessed man has *many* children, what does that say of a man who has *none*?

It is good to remember the context of this psalm—a song of worship for the nation of Israel. Their relationship with the Lord (and his blessings) related to dwelling in a land as a nation. Children were an integral part of that. In creation, the Lord had commanded humans to "be fruitful, multiply, fill the earth" (Genesis 1:28); and he had later promised to multiply Abraham's offspring into an uncountable number (Genesis 15:5). Further to that, practically speaking, a multitude of children was a necessity. Children grew to be warriors who protected the family and the people. They became farmers and shepherds and protected their parents against hunger in old age. The provision of such security indicated that God had blessed the nation.

When Jesus arrived, he turned things upside down. He arrived as the true son of Abraham. Of course, he did not have any children (which did not mean he was not blessed!). God's children would be those who were "born of the Spirit" (John 3:8). Jesus would be "the first-born among many brothers and sisters" (Romans 8:29). He came to save a spiritual nation of people made new, who would live on a new earth. Through Christ, God would birth a multitude of people that no one could count (Revelation 7:9).

The new reality brought by Jesus changed how God's people were to live. It transformed the command to fill the earth through procreation. God now commissions his people to fill the earth with disciples, people born of God (Matthew 28:18-20). That is why the apostle Paul wished that everyone might remain unmarried; it would allow undistracted devotion to the Lord (1 Corinthians 7:7, 32-35). For him, spiritual children were more important than biological ones.

Since the nature and calling of God's people has changed, so has the meaning of "blessed." If we operate with an underdeveloped concept of blessing, we fail to see the ways that God has blessed us. When we grasp the nature of Christ's kingdom, we begin to share his definition of "blessing."

We see what Jesus understood blessing to mean in his words to his disciples (Luke 6:20-22):

> Blessed are you who are poor,
>   because the kingdom of God is yours.
> Blessed are you who are hungry now,
>   because you will be filled.
> Blessed are you who weep now,
>   because you will laugh.
> Blessed are you when people hate you,
>   when they exclude you, insult you,
>   and slander your name as evil
>   because of the Son of Man.

In other words, material comforts in this world do not constitute our ultimate blessing. One's citizenship in Christ's kingdom is now the measure of such blessing.

As citizens of heaven, we are strangers on this earth. The citizens of this world will hate and mistreat us. We will weep. We will be hungry, empty, and poor. Our hearts will ache in painful dissatisfaction with this world as we long for our homeland.

Jesus says such persons are "blessed." Dissatisfaction with this world indicates that the kingdom of God is already ours (v 20). When that kingdom comes in its fullness, we will be full and laugh with joy.

Conversely, those who find their satisfaction in this life are not blessed. Jesus says "woe" to them because the most they will ever have is what they have now (v 24-26). One day, it will disappear, leaving them weeping and mourning in their hunger.

It is better to weep now and long for God's kingdom than to enjoy comfort now but have nothing once it's gone. That is a hard thing to hear in our suffering. It isn't easy to believe when a *good thing*—especially a child—is withheld from us. Such emptiness is a sharp, stinging reminder that this world is not as it should be. But as such, it is also a reminder that things will soon be as they should be.

The fact that you are mourning and asking, "Why won't Jesus bless us?" is a sign that he has blessed you already. You know Jesus to be a good Savior, a merciful Lord. This knowledge is what enables you to ask that question.

If you know Jesus, you've tasted his kingdom. Your question expresses your longing, which is a sign that his kingdom is yours. God will fill you. You will laugh.

Your arms are empty now, but your reward is great in heaven. Rejoice in that.

Go to God in prayer. Tell him about the pain of your emptiness. Tell him how dissatisfied you are with this broken-down old world. Tell him how much you want it all made new. Then ask him for the faith to believe that he has blessed you in Christ and that he will bless you forever.

REFLECT

- Which of these verses is the hardest to read?
- Which one helps you the most?

JOURNAL

11. LUKE 6:27-49
(Focus verses: 27-36)

What Do I Do with
My Anger?

After taking my wife home from the hospital following our third miscarriage, I went out to run errands. On the radio, a state congressman was being interviewed about a piece of legislation related to abortion. He said he didn't know why it was controversial because it only pertained to fetuses that were "just" within so many weeks of conception. The span he mentioned included the age of our recently miscarried baby.

My anger rose. This man was essentially saying that our baby didn't matter because it was only so old. There would be nothing wrong in killing our baby. In the end, it had no value. It angered me that this man could so casually dismiss the death of our baby. It maddened me to think that I was in a world where the value of a little one was up for a debate and where babies—*my* babies—were tossed around as a political issue.

My friend, the theologian Russell Moore, shares a similar story:

> *"While my wife experienced sadness, I toyed with,*
> *and eventually gave in to bitterness—a deep and*
> *hidden raised fist in the face of God. Once when*
> *I left our apartment after one of the miscarriages*
> *so I could get a prescription for Maria, I started*
> *the car only to hear on the radio the news that a*
> *scandalously immoral, unmarried female celebrity*
> *was pregnant—again. I scrunched up my face*
> *and breathed out a scoffing 'prayer': 'How's that*
> *just? This woman is pregnant while my sweet and*
> *godly wife, who would be an excellent mother,*
> *lies sobbing into her pillow upstairs.' I think*
> *that moment was perhaps the worst sin I've ever*
> *committed. I knew far better, but I was calling*
> *into question the goodness of my God to me."*

―――――

If you feel angry right now, you're not alone. Anger is a common response to miscarriage. It might appear as outrage at the neighbor who devalues your baby. It may be resentment toward the couple that just doesn't deserve their newborn. Sometimes, it is indignation toward the sovereign God who took away what you wanted.

Whatever the details, the question remains: what do we *do* with this anger?

Jesus tells us, "Love your enemies, do what is good to those who hate you, bless those who curse you, pray for those who mistreat you" (Luke 6:27-28). Suppose someone who dislikes you flaunts his children simply to provoke you. Or someone declares that your infertility is your own fault—as if it's evidence that you are cursed. Or a neighbor mistreats you by saying, "Well, it wasn't *really* a baby." Those are the kinds of enemies Jesus is talking about. So, what do you do?

To love someone means to genuinely desire and pursue their good, even at a cost to yourself. For the neighbors who flaunt their children, it may mean asking God to give you the grace to rejoice with them in those children— and looking for ways to serve them in all the difficulties and complications of childcare and parenting. For the one who implies you are cursed, it may look like asking Jesus to give them an accurate understanding of God's kingdom, in which those who weep are blessed. For the one who devalues your child, you might simply pray, "Father, please forgive them. They don't understand the value of a little child made in your image. Please open their eyes and help them cherish the littlest of people."

"Love ... do what is good ... bless ... pray for..." Those are difficult commands. They feel impossible when the object is someone who is hurting you. So, where do we find the ability to do them? How can it be possible to turn anger into love? We look to Jesus.

Our Lord does not ask of us anything that he is not willing to do himself. He tells us, "A disciple is not above his teacher, but everyone who is fully trained will be like his teacher" (v 40). Jesus' commands are nothing more than him telling us how to imitate him—how to walk the path he walked.

We ourselves were once enemies of God—hating God and neighbors, pronouncing curses, and mistreating others. Most people love only those who love them (v 32-34), but the love of God is not like the love of the world. "For he is gracious to the ungrateful and evil" (v 35). Instead of giving us what we deserve, Jesus loved us, did good to us, blessed us, and prayed for us.

When we are tempted to resent others, we can remember that we were once ungrateful and evil. But God was gracious toward us and saved us. We are now "children of the Most High" (v 35), who have the privilege of looking like our Father and following our Brother, Jesus.

When our hearts grow angry toward God for withholding something good, we can remember that he did not withhold the most significant good from us. He has given us himself. He has given us his Son. Through the death and resurrection of Jesus, we are adopted as God's children, who know a good Father.

Our new Brother, Jesus, knows what it's like to be hated, cursed, and mistreated. Even more, he knows what it's like to love his enemies and do them good, to bless and pray for them. This means he can help us to follow him in these situations. These things hurt, they really do. But they also bring us an opportunity to be like Jesus.

Read through the passage again and spend a moment reflecting on these truths. God loved you and sent his Son for you (John 3:16). Jesus loved you and gave himself for you (Ephesians 5:2). The Spirit is within you, guiding you into truth (John 16:13).

Are you angry? Ask for help. Ask Jesus to help you cherish the good news in your heart and bear good fruit (Luke 6:45). Then be merciful, just as your Father is merciful.

REFLECT

- Are you angry? Why? Who with?
- How can you behave like Jesus would to those people?

JOURNAL

Will Jesus Raise My Child from the Dead?

ach time my wife first suspected there was some-thing wrong with the pregnancy, we would pray. Like the centurion in Luke 7, we were full of faith that God could keep our baby alive. Like his messengers, we pleaded earnestly with Jesus. But, in our case, the result was different. There was no healing; there was only death.

Death hurts because it is so final. When we saw the baby on the ultrasound, settled and still on the bottom of the womb, we knew that nothing could be done. The baby would not revive. A living child would not be born.

I can't imagine the grief of the woman Jesus encoun-tered as he traveled to Nain. We learn she was a widow; she had no husband to provide for her. She had to depend on her only son to care for her. That son died. Now she had no one left. On the day she met Jesus, she was trav-eling with her son's open coffin to his burial place. Little wonder she was weeping as she went.

When Jesus saw her, his heart overflowed with compassion. He told her not to weep. He touched the coffin and commanded the young man to get up. Just like that. Imagine the woman's surprise and joy when her son really did sit up and begin to speak! He had been given back to her (Luke 7:15). Her tears of sorrow must have turned to tears of joy.

I've been to many funerals in my life, but I've never witnessed the deceased come back to life. I don't expect ever to see it. This miracle at Nain was a sign to demonstrate that Jesus is the Messiah and that he had come to conquer death. When I read this passage, I look forward to the resurrection to eternal life at Jesus' return. I look forward to the day when we will not only be given back to one another but also given by Jesus to our heavenly Father. I look forward to staying by his side forever.

But the thought of eternal life brings questions for us. Will Jesus raise my child from the dead? Is our little unseen baby safe in the arms of God? Those are difficult questions that many Christians answer differently. I want to briefly address what I believe the Bible teaches about infant salvation and how the resurrection gives me comfort.

Before I get there, I want to emphasize that it is difficult to speak with absolute certainty on this question. The Bible was not written to unborn persons who would die in the womb. It was written to reveal God's saving promises to those who can hear and understand them. What we, the living, do know is that God is perfect, just, good, and kind. Whatever he does in this area, as in all others, is right. Ultimately, we do not find our hope in the eternal fate of a miscarried child. We find it in the character of God—the God who sacrificed his Son to forgive our sins and raised him from the dead to give us eternal life.

I believe that miscarried babies are safe in the presence of God.[4] This is not because they do not have a sinful nature. Scripture is clear that we are all conceived in sin and hostile to God by nature (Psalm 51:5; Romans 8:7-8). But the Bible also suggests that God does not judge those who cannot know the truth of revelation in the same way he judges those who knowingly reject the truth.

Romans 1:18-21 upholds this idea. Paul states that people are without excuse, because God's glory is seen and understood in creation. God will condemn those who ignore this revelation. However, there are persons—such as infants in the womb and very young children—who do not possess the ability to see and understand. They are not physically able either to reject or accept what God has revealed. So, I believe this condemnation does not fall on them. Likewise, they are not able to understand and receive the revelation of God's grace in the gospel. God will not condemn them for not doing what they could not do. Nor will he judge them for sins they have not committed—and despite having a sinful nature, a miscarried child has not committed any sins. I believe that God

---

4 The basic outline of the arguments to follow originate in a sermon John Piper preached at the funeral of my friends' son, Owen, who lived for only ten minutes. You can find it at www.desiringgod.org/messages/funeral-meditation-for-owen.

instead unites them with Christ's saving righteousness in a way that we do not now understand.

That convinces me that miscarried children go to heaven at death and will be raised on the last day with glorious bodies. Like David, we can say of the children we have lost, "I'll go to him," even as we grieve the fact that "he will never return to me" (2 Samuel 12:23).

Nevertheless, I admit that Scripture says very little about this subject. That is why others land in different places on this question. But for all of us who believe in Jesus, the stories in Luke 7:1-17 give us hope. Jesus is full of compassion and justice. He reigns over death and all things. One day, he will raise his people from the dead and—whatever the extent of our sorrows—wipe every tear from our eyes.

As you mourn the death of your child, take a moment to think about the day that Jesus will wipe your tears away. Set your hope on that final day, when Jesus will appear to save us from all sorrow, sin, and death.

REFLECT

- What's your response when you read these stories? How do you feel? What do you think?
- What, practically speaking, could help you hope as well as grieve?

JOURNAL

What Should I Do
with My Confusion?

A friend told me that miscarriage was the first time he realized the world was not safe. Having been raised in a healthy Christian home, he attended a sound church and had a happy marriage. When he and his wife learned they were pregnant, it seemed like the last piece of the puzzle. Life was perfect. Then, unexpectedly, miscarriage struck. My friend's first experience with suffering left him confused and full of questions. *I've been faithful to God, so why this pain? Isn't Jesus a Savior? Why would he allow this? Can I trust him in the future?*

If such confusion describes you, please know that you are not the first to feel this way.

Imagine the confidence John the Baptist had felt at Jesus' baptism. He'd seen the Spirit descend and rest on Jesus. John knew that this sign would indicate the Son of God. So, he declared Jesus to be "the Lamb of God, who takes away the sin of the world!" (John 1:29-34).

The arrival of the Messiah must have been thrilling.

Like the rest of Israel, John and his disciples expected the Messiah to restore the nation to its former glory. The nations—Rome in particular—would be judged. Israel would be independent again and foreign occupants removed. God's Chosen One, the Messiah, would replace the wicked King Herod.

So, imagine John's confusion now. His disciples are telling John about Jesus' miraculous signs—including raising a man from the dead (Luke 7:18). But John has been put in prison (3:20). Herod is still king. Rome still occupies the land. If Jesus is the Messiah, why haven't things been set right?

John sent two of his disciples to ask Jesus, "Are you the one who is to come, or should we expect someone else?" (7:18-20). John was asking the same kind of question my friend asked. *Why am I experiencing this hardship if Jesus is the Savior who came to right all wrongs?*

I wonder what sort of answer John hoped to receive. I wonder how you would like Jesus to answer you.

———

To answer John's question, Jesus pointed him to his works. "The blind receive their sight, the lame walk, those with leprosy are cleansed, the deaf hear, the dead are raised, and the poor are told the good news" (v 22). These were the types of miracles that Isaiah had proclaimed would accompany God's kingdom (Isaiah 35:5-6). Jesus' performance of these signs was evidence enough that he was the one who had been promised.

But the last bit of Jesus' reply is curious. "And blessed is the one who isn't offended by me" (Luke 7:23).

We might wonder how anyone could be offended by Jesus. But many were. Jesus' healing miracles often involved contact with the unclean and outcasts. He touched lepers and dead people, which the law forbade. The religious leaders assumed that physical impairments resulted from some egregious sin, yet Jesus showed sufferers mercy. He condemned the religious elite as hypocrites while he offered the kingdom to the poor. How could this man be the Messiah? The idea was scandalous. Who would believe such a thing?

The blessed—the blessed would believe such a thing. In Jesus' kingdom, the blessed are those whose preconceived notions of the kingdom do not blind them to its arrival. The King had not arrived with political revolution and military might but as a humble Galilean. Jesus socialized with sinners and touched the unclean. He allowed himself to be arrested and crucified. That did not look like what people expected. Nevertheless, the eyes of faith see Jesus for who he is—the Messiah, who ushers in the kingdom of God.

Jesus' answer offers John both comfort and challenge. "The poor are told the good news." John, sitting in prison, more than qualifies as "the poor." The good news of the kingdom is for him! That should comfort you too, friend. You've suffered the loss of a valuable thing—a child. In this way, you are genuinely impoverished. The good news of salvation is for such as you—for those who weep (Luke 6:21).

But Jesus has also offered a gracious warning: *Don't be offended by me if I do not meet your expectations.* Many would reject Jesus because he didn't look like the king they wanted. They would not receive the blessing of the kingdom. But those who accepted Jesus, judging him not by their own desires but by what he actually did and said, would be blessed and brought into his kingdom.

Right now, friend, your life may not look like what you expected. You might be confused about what Jesus is up to. I've been there too. It's hard, and it hurts. If this miscarriage has left you confused, look again at Jesus. Keep reading the Gospel of Luke. See what Jesus has done. Through signs and wonders, Jesus proved that he is God's Chosen One. He is a friend to those who mourn. You can trust him.

REFLECT

- What expectations did you have that have been squashed now?
- Do you trust Jesus as he is?

JOURNAL

How Do I Care
for My Wife?

Fathers and mothers experience miscarriage differently. The mother was pregnant; a child was conceived and lived inside her. Physical, hormonal, and mental changes happened as her body and mind adapted, preparing to protect, nourish, and carry this little life.

Then that little one died within her, and the child had to exit her body. That process can have consequences ranging from aches and pains to paralyzing cramps to recovery from surgery. She may have temporary physical limitations. Her body changes again as it returns to its former (not pregnant) state. Her mind is readjusting as well. From the time she learned of this pregnancy, she was looking ahead—to the birth, to bringing the baby home, to meeting grandpa and grandma, and so on. But now, all of that is gone. That may result in depression or a season of spiritual turmoil.

Don't forget that your wife is more than mental and

physical—she is a spiritual being. Like you, she is a sinner. Physical and mental affliction can impact our spiritual strength and focus. They decrease our ability and willingness to resist temptation. Depending on her temperament, your wife may be prone to anger or despair, lashing out or withholding affection. Perhaps you've seen her sin more clearly in this period—and you may have been on the receiving end of it!

You're also suffering, but not in the same way. You have had no direct physical symptoms—no cramping, no surgical procedure, no physical recovery time. Barring other limitations, this leaves you with the physical strength to serve your wife. You may also have greater strength to resist temptation. But even so, you too are naturally a sinner. You may feel unappreciated and begin to shrink back. Bitterness may grow at undeserved insults. Your sin may tempt you to be ungracious with her sin. All of this raises the question of how to make sure you are caring well for your wife.

———

Jesus loved women. In our reading, we see that a group of women followed Jesus, providing for him out of their own means (Luke 8:2-3). Luke's Gospel often highlights and emphasizes the role of women in the story of Jesus. Today's passage recalls how this looked on one occasion.

A Pharisee had invited Jesus to a meal in his home. Such meals were semi-public events that others could come and observe. Having a celebrated teacher at the table—one who people claimed was a prophet—would undoubtedly help the host's status!

But as the meal progressed, there was an unexpected (and embarrassing!) interruption. A sinful woman knelt behind Jesus, weeping over his feet and drying them with her hair. She kissed his feet and anointed them with expensive ointment.

It must have taken a lot to bring this woman to Jesus' feet. She was a notorious sinner. She knew it. Everyone in town knew it. She knew everyone knew it. She had likely been shunned, insulted, spit on, and abused by many people, including some who were right there at the Pharisee's house. She was a sinner and a sufferer. To go to this party meant making herself vulnerable to more suffering.

She had traveled to that meal knowing that every eye in the room would be on her, judging her, condemning her—every eye, that is, but one. Her faith in that one made her willing to go and honor him.

The Pharisee, of course, was horrified. In his thoughts, he condemned both Jesus and the woman. *If Jesus were a prophet, he would know he should not even touch her.*

But her faith was well-placed: Jesus did not share the Pharisee's attitude. Instead he showed mercy. He noticed the woman and welcomed her touch. He served her by speaking up in her defense. He affirmed her love and comforted her with forgiveness.

Jesus' response—to show mercy, notice, serve, affirm, comfort—is a helpful model for how we should care for our wives when their suffering or their sin is especially bitter. As you reflect on this passage, spend some time thinking and praying about how you might love your wife as Jesus does.

Show mercy to your wife. She is a sinner and a sufferer. She is and has been in a vulnerable place. Do not serve her expecting something in return. Do not return sin for sin. Overlook offense. Forgive her as Christ has forgiven you.

Notice your wife. How is she doing? Is she in physical pain or discomfort? Stressed, depressed, or despondent? Is she spiritually struggling or thriving?

Serve your wife. Be a good listener when she wants to talk. Seek to discern what she needs. Ask advice from her friends and mature women in your church. Make use of the suggestions in the appendix by Nate Wilbert at the back of this book (page 186).

Affirm your wife. In Christ, she is truly a child of God. He forgives her sins through Jesus' death and resurrection. God loves her perfectly and eternally. This miscarriage is not a sign that she has done anything wrong; it is not her fault. Remind her of the reasons why you love and cherish her. Affirm her grief and sorrow: she suffered the death of a child, and it is right to be sad. Affirm her choices and responses to the miscarriage. There is no timetable that she must follow. It is different for everyone.

Comfort your wife. Remind her of God's goodness. Pray with her. Read the Psalms together. Tend to her. Order in her favorite meals. Eat them together while watching her favorite movies. With her permission, invite close friends for a short visit.

Jesus is not only our Savior; he is an example of one who served others even as he suffered. Ask him for the grace, strength, and wisdom to serve your wife. Ask with confidence, because Jesus loves to help us in our need.

REFLECT

- What does your wife have in common with the woman in the story?
- Who in the story do you have most in common with?

JOURNAL

(Focus verses: 40-56)

Can I Trust Jesus' Timing?

The term "family planning" is used today to mean "the ability to achieve desired family size and spacing between the birth of children." I've often wondered what biblical characters would think of the term. Today there are many means of preventing conception and, unfortunately, of voluntarily ending a pregnancy. But as we know, becoming and remaining pregnant can be a heartbreaking frustration. For all our science, the successful birth of a baby is still in God's hands.

We make lots of plans around having children. We might plan to have children at the same time as our siblings so the cousins can grow up together. We might want siblings close in age so they can be playmates and friends. We'd like aging parents and grandparents to be able to meet their grandchild. Those are good plans—but miscarriage and infertility frustrate them. We end up asking whether we can really trust God's timing.

Today's reading makes the answer to that question clear.

It starts with a man named Jairus, who had found Jesus and fallen at his feet, pleading with him to come to his house. His only daughter was sick. If Jesus didn't heal her soon, she would die. The timing was urgent. Imagine Jairus's relief when Jesus agreed to go with him.

Jairus may have grown nervous as they went. The crowds were nearly crushing Jesus and likely slowing his progress. Imagine his alarm when Jesus stopped altogether. He asked who had touched him. *Why does it matter?* Jairus must have thought. As Jesus' disciples pointed out, he was surrounded by crowds—everyone was touching him!

But Jesus insisted on completing his search. Someone had touched him in faith. Power had gone out from him to heal them. Jesus would wait right there until that person came forward.

At last, a woman, trembling and afraid, fell at Jesus' feet. She explained that she had touched him because she had been bleeding for twelve years. She had found Jesus in the crowd and got close enough to touch the end of his robe. When she touched him, she had been healed.

Jesus patiently listened to her account. He assured her that her faith in him had saved her. He told her to go in peace.

Finally, Jairus must have thought. *Great! Now we can get moving!* But just then, someone from his house arrived with bad news. Jesus didn't need to come anymore. Jairus's daughter had died.

———

If you were Jairus, what would you be thinking? I'd wail, "I was here first! If you hadn't waited to learn who touched you, we might have arrived at my house in time!" I'd ask, "The woman was healed already, so why did you have to stop and talk to her?" I'd wonder, "Why did her faith save her, but my faith didn't save my daughter?" This pause in the journey had cost Jairus his little girl. It seemed like the worst possible timing.

But Jesus told Jairus to believe that he would still save his daughter. They completed the journey to Jairus's house and, to the amazement of all the household, Jesus raised the little girl from the dead.

If Jesus had arrived in time, he would have healed a sick girl. But due to the delay caused by attending to the healed woman, Jesus did something better than heal the sick. He raised the dead. What seemed like a tragic pause in Jesus' timing resulted in a more remarkable display of Jesus' glory.

———

Isn't it just like God to work like that?

The Israelites complained that their hasty exit from Egypt left them to starve in the wilderness. If God had timed it better, perhaps they could have packed supplies. But God's "bad timing" resulted in a glorious display of his miraculous provision of manna.

Mary and Joseph had to travel a long distance when

Mary was pregnant—perhaps heavily pregnant. That was not only inconvenient; it was also dangerous! Yet God used this "bad timing" to fulfill his promise of a Savior born in Bethlehem.

Mary and Martha sent urgent news to Jesus. Their brother Lazarus was seriously sick. But when Jesus heard this, he decided to wait two more days before leaving. When he finally arrived, Lazarus had been dead for over four days. Both Martha and Mary said, "Lord, if you had been here, my brother wouldn't have died" (John 11:21, 32). In response, Jesus not only taught them about the resurrection but also demonstrated it by raising Lazarus from the dead. Jesus' "bad timing" resulted in a miracle which proved that Jesus is the resurrection and the life for all who believe.

God is no less sovereign over the timing of our miscarriages than he was over the timing of these events. This "bad timing" isn't because he was caught by surprise. (He wasn't.) It isn't because he was unable to stop it. (He was.) No, the timing of our sorrows is because Jesus loves us and wants to show us his glory in ways that we could not imagine. I don't know how God is revealing his glory in your situation, but we can be sure he is. Whether today, a decade from now, or in eternity, I trust that you will marvel at what God has done.

God revealed his glory to me in simple and surprising ways. You'll read about some of these in the last half of this book. He showed me the weakness of my flesh—fear, doubt, physical limitations. Then he mercifully provided comfort, assurance, and strength. He used the suffering to reveal my sin—impatience, pride, self-centeredness. Then he graciously brought me to Jesus, who forgives, accepts, and loves me.

That does not mean that our suffering doesn't hurt. The Israelites were hungry and thirsty. Mary was uncomfortable on the road to Bethlehem. Jesus wept real tears over Lazarus' death. Miscarriage brings deep pain.

God's sovereignty does not mean we forget our sorrows and instantly cheer up. But it does mean that we can trust him. Through our tears and heartbreak, we can trust him to save us and to do all things well.

REFLECT

- What has been hard about the timing of things for you?
- When in the past has bad timing proved to be good timing?

JOURNAL

What Do I Really Believe about Jesus?

"Who do you say that I am?" That's the question Jesus posed to his disciples (Luke 9:20). My initial response is "That's easy!" I've attended church my whole life, taught the Bible for over 20 years, and pastored churches for almost as long. I earned a master's degree in biblical and theological studies. It's no effort for me to rattle off the facts.

But when life circumstances take a turn for the worse, answering that question somehow becomes much more difficult. When faced with suffering and loss, the question becomes not "Who do I say he is?" but "Who do I *really* believe he is?"

I've been in places where darkness seemed to blot out any sign of God's light. His promises felt empty and distant. I wondered, is Jesus really my Savior? Does he see me? Does he have mercy for me, or is it only for other people? Does he offer any hope? Do I really believe that Jesus is who I say he is?

I love today's passage because in it, Jesus gives his disciples some hard-to-swallow truths about who he is. I also love it because he is revealing himself to men whose hearts will fail to believe and confess it when he's carried off to execution. Jesus loves such men—those like Peter and me, whose hearts are fickle and whose faith is weak. These are the people he lived and died and rose for. These are the people he reveals himself to.

Peter answered Jesus' question correctly—"God's Messiah" (v 20). "Messiah" means "Anointed One." It's the title of the promised one who, God foretold, would come to fulfill all his promises. But what Jesus reveals about the Messiah is unexpected: "It is necessary that the Son of Man suffer many things and be rejected by the elders, chief priests, and scribes, be killed, and be raised the third day" (v 22). He is the King—but not the one Peter expects.

———

Jesus is the rejected King. Israel's religious elite—the elders, chief priests, and scribes—were the people you would have expected to spot the Messiah first! But they rejected him from beginning to end. Why? Because he didn't look like what they expected. They expected power; he looked weak. They expected something big; he made himself little. They could not see his glory because his glory was hidden.

Peter, John, and James saw Jesus' glory on the mountain (v 28-32). A voice from heaven thundered, "This is my Son, the Chosen One; listen to him!" (v 35). Peter offered to build shelters for Jesus, Moses, and Elijah, perhaps hoping they'd stay there for good. But Peter misunderstood. This dazzling glory wasn't the kind of glory Jesus was born to reveal on earth. Jesus displayed his glory in suffering, voluntary humiliation, and death.

Miscarriage is a hidden thing. You likely haven't seen your little one, except perhaps on a computer screen. Maybe only you and the mother know about it. God's glory can seem hidden here too. Where is his greatness, mercy, and love in this pain? We can't see it. It looks and feels weak, pitiful, and humiliating.

That is, it looks like Jesus.

———

Jesus is the killed King. "It is necessary that the Son of Man suffer many things and ... be killed." *Necessary* is an interesting word. It's not that they lynched Jesus, and the Father found a way to make it work in his plan. It's not as if Jesus chose this option out of a dozen presented. No, the Messiah's murder was necessary. He had to die.

The apostle Paul would tell us that the cross of Christ is foolishness and weakness to the world (1 Corinthians 1:18-25). Perhaps that's one reason why Jesus told his disciples that whoever welcomes a little child welcomes him—and if they welcome him, they welcome the Father (Luke 9:46-48). Little children are weak, needing parents to protect and provide for them. Little children lack wisdom, needing to be taught. Here is a picture of foolishness and weakness—but Jesus says that foolishness and weakness are what you need to be able to welcome. That, after all, is what the cross is like.

———

Jesus is the risen King. Jesus had to be killed because he had to be raised. You can't have a resurrection without a death. Rising from the dead, Jesus put death to death, canceled sin, and crushed Satan's head. That's good news because he did those things for us—those afflicted by Satan and enslaved to sin, who feel the sting of death. When we read about Jesus healing a demon-possessed boy (v 42), we're getting a glimpse of how his power is for us. One day, Jesus will return and rebuke all that assails us. He'll set us free. Forever.

We live in this world—one full of pain, sorrow, and loss—as we wait for the next one. Jesus says if we want to rejoice when he returns in glory, then we need to be willing to follow him in death now (v 23-27). That's a hard calling. But, he promises, if we lose our life in following him now, we'll save it.

Miscarriage is a cross to bear. It's a suffering that we must surrender to God in faith. But Jesus promises that it is *better* to have him than to have a nursery full of children. I don't mean to sound trite; I say it because it's true. We know that there is glory, life, and joy on the other side of whatever cross we must bear.

That's who Jesus is—the king who takes the path of rejection and death to eternal glory. God loves us enough to make us like Jesus (Romans 8:29), so our path is in some measure the same. Miscarriage reminds me that I have not got to the glory part yet. I'm still trudging my way through rejection and death—as are you. But resurrection glory is coming, friend. That is who Jesus is.

REFLECT

- Who says what about Jesus in the passage you have read?
- Is following Jesus worth it?

JOURNAL

Are We Making
Too Much of This?

Our third miscarriage occurred late enough that my wife was able to be induced to labor and deliver the child. We chose this to avoid dilation and curettage. After enduring painful contractions, she finally delivered. I called the nurse.

While we waited for her to arrive, I saw the body of our tiny, palm-sized child lying on the bed in a pool of blood and fluids. Everything in me wanted to pick up and hold our child. That was my child. My child, even in death, should not be lying there alone and unattended. But I didn't. What would the nurse think if she walked in to find me holding a bloody fetus? I felt ashamed of mourning this death.

The next day, before returning home, we asked to see the baby. One nurse politely discouraged us. At this stage in pregnancy, the baby didn't have a hardened skeletal structure. With the loss of fluids, a day later, the body wouldn't look much like a baby. Shame hit me again for wanting to hold my child—but this time we insisted.

We each held the little body in a cupped hand. We could count the intricate fingers on the tiny hands at the end of fragile arms. This was a baby, our baby—fearfully and wonderfully made.

When we were ready, I called the nurses' station. I asked the nurse for someone to take our baby. She explained that no one was available and that it might be a while. I told her that we were about to go home and needed someone to get the baby. She asked why we wanted someone to get the baby. "Because..." I stuttered, looking for words. "Our baby died."

She didn't know. *She's probably annoyed with me,* I thought. *They're busy, and we're a nuisance.* Once again, there was shame over mourning this baby.

We had a funeral home pick up the baby so that we could bury our child. The following week, our family huddled in the cold around a small box on a table in the children's section of the cemetery. I read Scripture and prayed. The funeral director stood several yards away. I imagined that he, too, was annoyed with us, impatient to get back to "real funerals." There it was—shame, again, over mourning our baby's death.

———

There are many opportunities for shame in miscarriage. Family and friends didn't see the baby and may have been unaware of the pregnancy. It's easy to wonder if this child even "counts" as a real child. Or whether it's ok to have a funeral service, to bury the child (when that's possible). Is it acceptable to take time away for mourning, to remember the anniversary of the death? Will others see my remembrance as an intrusion into their otherwise happy lives? Might we be making too much of this?

If you've experienced this sort of shame, I wonder how today's reading struck you. A would-be disciple agrees to follow Jesus with one request—"First let me go bury my father" (Luke 9:59). The proposal seems reasonable. The burial of parents was one of the highest religious duties a Jew had. But Jesus answers, "Let the dead bury their own dead, but you go and spread the news of the kingdom of God" (v 60). Another requested something far less than burial—to say goodbye to his family. But Jesus answers, "No one who puts his hand to the plow and looks back is fit for the kingdom of God" (v 62).

This passage is a classic "hard saying" of Jesus. Its main point is not how to deal with miscarriage. But we might be tempted to apply it to miscarriage by reasoning from the greater to lesser. The first man wanted to bury his *father*—a living, full-grown adult. If Jesus forbade that, how much more would he forbid the burial of an unborn child! The other man wanted to say goodbye to his family—the household of living people with whom he ate, talked, and lived. If Jesus forbade looking back at such a family, how much more would he forbid looking back at the anniversary of a miscarriage! Such a reading might lead us to believe that burying and remembering an unborn child is incompatible with following Jesus. But such a reading would be wrong.

Jesus' first remark is in the context of emphasizing the priority of the kingdom. The burial and mourning of a father could be a year-long process. Making this his first response to Jesus indicates that the man is likely making an excuse for not immediately following him. Jesus' second remark highlights the same point: the kingdom of God takes priority over all things and all relationships. So, the application to a miscarriage might be this: *If I quit following Christ because we lost a baby, then I haven't understood the kingdom of God.* Jesus is saying that where there is a choice between him and something else, he must always come first. But that is not the choice before us when we think about mourning our losses.

Jesus did not forbid burial and mourning any more than he prohibits owning a bed (9:58) or preparing for a trip (10:4). If we believe that miscarriage is the death of a child (see chapter 2), then a service, burial, grieving period, and times to remember are just as appropriate as they are with any other death. Jesus stood at Lazarus' grave and wept without shame, despite knowing he would raise him from the dead only minutes later. Your baby was just as much of a person as Lazarus—just as known and loved by the God who formed him or her in the womb. Provided your loss does not take priority over Jesus, you're not making too much of it.

"Blessed are those who mourn, for they will be comforted" (Matthew 5:4). Jesus is there with us in our mourning. He sees no shame in it. And he promises that one day he will bring our grieving to an end.

REFLECT

- How much have you made of your miscarriage? Too much? Too little?
- How can you keep the kingdom of God as your priority while you grieve?

JOURNAL

Is It Ok to
Ask for Help?

I found attending church after miscarriage an uncomfortable experience. Women would make their way to my wife to express their condolences and ask how she was doing. Most men simply gave either a greeting or a handshake, engaging in conversation as though nothing had happened. A few expressed their sorrow for our loss. Only one man hugged me. When men did broach the subject of the miscarriage, it was generally to ask how my wife was doing. Few, if any, asked how I was.

Many hold an unspoken belief that miscarriage is the mother's loss, not the father's. Fathers don't carry babies, and so, it seems, they aren't expected to grieve. If they do mourn, it shouldn't be as deeply as the mother. The father's role is to care for his wife and, if applicable, the rest of the family. He should need no time to tend to his own heart.

With this mindset, a father may attempt to take on all the household duties as his wife recovers. He tries to carry alone what was once a two-person job. It rarely works out smoothly—in fact, it often looks like a comedy film about a father left alone with the kids. We shouldn't expect to succeed. God gave us our wives for a reason—we *need* them. When your wife is recovering from a miscarriage, you notice your need for her everywhere. That need does not go away while she rests and recovers. So, you have two choices—go it alone or ask for help.

Before the advent of smartphones and map apps, we had to use paper maps or ask people for directions. There was a common joke that men would *never* stop to ask for directions. They would sooner run out of gas than admit they were lost. Such behavior often stems from an unhealthy view of manhood that forbids admitting weakness. We wonder if it is ok to ask for help, to tell others what we need. Isn't that selfish? Weak? Unspiritual?

Trying to do alone what I cannot do alone is not only proud or foolish; it fails to serve others and honor God. God did not intend for us to be alone. He designed us to display his glory in a community. When I refuse to ask for help—whether in caring for my heart or in doing household chores—I fail to glorify God. Moreover, I end up neglecting those I'm trying to serve. I even harm myself by refusing to ask for care. All that because I am too proud to ask for help. Today's reading is full of reasons to ask for help—reasons that I, and perhaps you, need to hear.

Jesus tells the story of a man robbed and beaten as he traveled from Jerusalem to Jericho. Two men saw him and passed by, keeping their distance. But a Samaritan man stopped and showed compassion. When Jesus concludes the parable, he asks which of the three men proved to be a neighbor. The answer, we learn, is "the one who showed mercy to him" (Luke 10:37). To be a neighbor is to see someone in need, have compassion, and care for them.

The Samaritan showed compassion. He cared for the man himself—tending his wounds, bringing him to an inn, staying the night with him. He also paid the inn-keeper and asked him to take care of the man until he returned. He helped in every way he could.

You might be thinking, "That's what I'm doing! I'm showing compassion to my wife and family!" That's true, I hope. But have you ever thought of how other people might be a neighbor to you? We don't naturally see ourselves as the wounded man lying in the road. But sometimes that is who we are in this story. Sometimes, we are the ones who need help.

You and I are not the only neighbors in the world. God calls every human to be a neighbor. Did the injured man refuse the Samaritan's assistance? Of course not. But that's what I'm doing when I don't ask others to help. I deny them the opportunity to be a neighbor. Now I'm failing to love two neighbors—the one I'm trying to help while overwhelmed and the one who could help me.

Once, before a meal, Jesus began to wash his disciples' feet. When Jesus arrived at the feet of Peter, the disciple objected, "You will never wash my feet!" Jesus replied, "If I don't wash you, you have no part with me" (John 13:1-10).

The starting point of the Christian life is trusting in Christ to serve you—to save you through his death and resurrection. Being served by Jesus is a non-negotiable; before we can be servants of Jesus, we must be served by Jesus. One of the ways that Jesus continues to serve us is through the gift of neighbors. He did not provide us with neighbors merely so that we could serve them. He also gave us neighbors so that they could serve us. When we refuse to ask for help, we refuse to be served by Jesus.

Our Lord teaches us how to ask for help. "Whenever you pray, say, Father ... Give us each day our daily bread" (Luke 11:3). Even with a provision as mundane as bread, we're to ask for it. We're to ask for help, seek help, and knock on doors to get help because we have a heavenly Father who is eager and willing to give us good things (11:5-13).

Jesus did not come for the healthy and the righteous but for the sick and sinful (5:31-32). He came to be merciful to the weak and needy. Why not ask God to help you right now? Whether it's your broken heart, spiritual dryness, or physical exhaustion, tell him your needs. Ask him to provide neighbors to help you. Ask him for the humility to ask for help. He's more than happy to help.

REFLECT

- Are you willing to be served by Jesus through the help of your neighbors?
- What help do you need? Who could you ask?

JOURNAL

Is This Miscarriage
a Curse?

"You have *five* children? Wow. You are certainly blessed." I cringe when I hear that sort of comment. I know it is well intended. I know it is true to a certain degree. But I also know how these words are heard and applied by those walking through miscarriage and infertility.

For parents with living children, they seem to diminish the lost child's value. *It's not that big a loss. You have others, after all!* Worse, for those living with infertility, those words overheard may land on you like a curse. You begin to reason it out: *"Blessing" is found in a multitude of children. We're unable to have children. Therefore, we are not blessed. The opposite of "blessed" is "cursed." That's us—we're cursed.*

That internal dialogue captures the mindset that was prevalent in Jesus' day. We hear it in the words a woman shouted to Jesus: "Blessed is the womb that bore you and the one who nursed you!" (Luke 11:27). If having a child is a blessing, she reasoned, then how much more blessed must be the woman who birthed the Messiah! And she was right—to a certain degree. Elizabeth did declare to Mary, "Blessed are you among women!" (1:42).

Once again, though, Jesus shows us that the kingdom of God uses a different metric than the world. His response opens with "rather," contradicting her answer. No, he says, "Blessed are those who hear the word of God and keep it" (11:28). The woman thinks blessedness is seen in the externals—in this case, children. But the metric of the kingdom is quite the opposite. It measures blessedness by what's inside: a heart that knows and loves God.

The woman, though she thinks she's honoring Jesus, actually aligns herself with the Pharisees. They judged a person's blessedness by what they could see on the outside—ritual washing, meticulous tithing, front-row seats in worship, and greetings that communicated high status. Jesus condemned them in strong language—"Woe to you Pharisees!" (v 42). While they presented well externally, their insides rotted and stank. They neither knew nor obeyed God. They were not, by Jesus' definition, blessed.

We mourn miscarriage and pregnancy loss because they are part of the brokenness of the world. Death should not be. So we grieve. But this loss, and the absence of children, is no indication that you are specially cursed.

Child-bearing is an external condition, available only to some. Like external rule-keeping, it indicates nothing about one's heart. But knowing God's word and keeping it is a possibility for anyone who will open their Bible.

And what good news it has for those who will read and receive it by faith.

It can hurt when you can't have the status symbols the world values. But it is soul-crushing when you don't have the status symbols that many in the church value. Unfortunately, Christians often think like the woman in the crowd: the more children you have, the more blessed you are.

But don't be concerned by those who measure blessedness by anything other than Jesus' metric. Jesus reminds us in 12:4-5 that the worst people can do is kill us. But God is greater than people—he controls what happens after death. We should fear him. Blessed are those who fear the Lord.

Now Jesus brings the good news—"Don't be afraid" (v 7). We *should* fear the one who can send us to hell after death (v 5). But God does *not* send to hell those who hear the gospel and follow Christ. God notices every sparrow, the most worthless of birds in the eyes of the world (v 6). But he values those who follow his Son so much that he numbers the hairs on their heads (v 7). Blessed are those whose hairs the Father counts.

People of this world worry about this life—what they will eat, what they will wear, how many children they will have. Jesus tells us not to worry about such things: "For life is more than food and the body more than clothing" (v 23). Friend, life is more than babies. And besides, your worry cannot change a single thing. Blessed are those who look to God in faith.

We're called to concern ourselves with something better: with the kingdom of God. Our heart follows our treasure (v 34). And if we treasure the kingdom, our hearts will find fulness in the end. We need not fear, because the Father delights in giving us the kingdom (v 32)—and everything else we need (v 31). Blessed are those who become poor because the kingdom is their treasure.

Miscarriage should not cause you to believe that God cursed you. Experiencing a tragedy does not mean you're worse in God's sight than others (13:1-5). Instead, miscarriage should make us long for the end of the curse brought on the whole world by sin. Jesus removed that curse in his death. He showed us the end of death in his resurrection. That's the kingdom we're waiting for at his return—a blessed realm of life. Blessed are those who repent and find eternal life in Christ.

Miscarriage reminds us why we wait. Jesus commands us to wait like servants waiting for their master's return (12:35-48). Blessed are those who hear the word of God and keep it. Blessed are you, the waiting, for the Father delights to give you his kingdom.

REFLECT

- What blessings has God given you, according to what you have read here?
- How will you treasure God's kingdom above all else?

JOURNAL

What about Sex?

Between conception and miscarriage, a host of physical and chemical changes took place in your wife's body. She may have experienced morning sickness—vomiting more times than you could count—or a variety of other aches, pains, and general discomfort. And that's just before the miscarriage. During it, she may have endured horrific cramping or intolerable contractions. Now her body is readjusting to its pre-pregnancy state.

You, on the other hand, experienced none of those physical changes in your body. Barring other conditions, everything is probably running as expected—including your libido. You and your body may be beginning to wonder, when do we get to have sex?

Many of the changes described above originate or occur in one of the most intimate areas of your wife's body. It is no coincidence that sexual intercourse involves the very same location. Before you ask your wife for sex, pause for a moment to consider what is best for her. Jesus calls husbands to sacrifice their comfort for the sake of serving their wives (Ephesians 5:25-28).

We find an excellent example of Jesus' love in Luke 13:10-17. Luke describes a woman who was listening to Jesus teach in the synagogue. An evil spirit had disabled her for more than 18 years, bending her over so that she could not straighten up at all. Imagine the suffering she endured—terrible pain, the inability to sit or lie down comfortably, the cruelty of people. If she had been married, her husband had likely divorced her. Children would taunt her. People would cross the street to avoid contact with her. How would Jesus respond?

———

Jesus saw her. He understood her condition. The Messiah knew what she needed and was determined to do her good. "Woman," he called out, "you are free of your disability" (v 12).

Do you see your wife as Jesus saw this woman? Do you understand her condition? You're not Jesus, so this will require a conversation with your wife. It would be best if you learned from her what she needs and if she is ready. Is she physically healed? Is she able to have sex? Has her doctor said intercourse is safe? Will physical intimacy cause her pain? Does she desire to make love? Is she emotionally ready?

Don't ask those questions merely to get clearance to make love. Ask them because you're determined to do her good whatever the answer.

———

Jesus touched her. A woman with a full-body deformity was not likely a person 1st-century Jews were clamoring to touch. Where could you touch her? Would you become unclean? Would the demon go into you? How could you embrace her? If she knew touch, it was likely only from someone pushing her aside in the street.

Yet, Jesus "laid his hands on her." He did not touch her like those who shoved her aside at the well. Or those who pushed past her at a market stall. Or those who tried to keep any touch to the minimum as they passed her in the synagogue. Jesus had the gentle hands of a kind servant. His touch was not for his own sake but for hers.

Will you touch your wife like Jesus touched this woman? Sexual intercourse is the most vulnerable and sacred of all human touch. God designed it as a physical expression of love for the other. Determine that sexual touch will only occur when it is suitable for her. Let your touch be that of a kind servant, not that of a greedy narcissist.

———

Jesus valued her. The leader of the synagogue objected to the healing because it was the Sabbath. There were six days when Jesus could do such work with his hands, but the Sabbath was not one of them. Jesus condemned him as a hypocrite. Everyone there would have used their hands on the Sabbath to untie an ox or donkey to lead it to water. Yet this leader claimed that Jesus should not spiritually unbind this woman. He valued her less than a beast of burden.

But Jesus loved the woman as himself. She was a "daughter of Abraham," part of his own family. Satan had captured her. It was Jesus' familial duty to free and restore her. And so he did.

Will you value your wife as Jesus valued this woman? Will you love her body as your own flesh? Do you see how the fall has afflicted her? Because the world is broken, death visited her body. Are her healing and restoration your priority? It was not a comfortable moment to be opposed by the leader of the synagogue. But Jesus valued her comfort ahead of his own. Will you love your wife in the same way?

Go to God in prayer, seeking wisdom. Ask him to fill you with patience, kindness, and gentleness. Ask him to fill your heart with genuine love so that you love your wife as yourself. Express to him your physical desires and ask for self-control. The love of a husband for his wife is to be a picture of Christ's love for his church. God delights to honor his Son, so you can be confident he'll answer such prayer.

REFLECT

- Before the miscarriage, how did your sex life show your wife that you value her?
- What's the best way of loving and valuing her today?

JOURNAL

Does My Grief Make Me Useless to Jesus?

All of our miscarriages have occurred while I've been a pastor. In that role, I've experienced heaps of expectations about who I am, how I am, and what I can do. Some of those presumptions came from others, but too many I put on myself.

I'm often tempted to believe that I should "have it all together." A good pastor is one whose faith doesn't falter and whose heart is perpetually happy. He never has drooping hands or weak knees in need of strengthening. So I began to believe there was no room in my life for grief and exhaustion. I couldn't afford to be depressed or overwhelmed. God had called me to serve Jesus and his church, and service, I thought, flows from strength, energy, and boundless joy. I couldn't serve Jesus from a place of weakness, tiredness, and grief. Or could I?

Jesus never fails to turn my expectations on their head. He's precisely the opposite of what I expect a shepherd to be. Isaiah didn't foretell an Unflagging Leader but a

Suffering Servant—despised, rejected, and acquainted with grief (Isaiah 53). He got hungry and thirsty (Matthew 4:2; John 19:28). He got "worn out" (John 4:6). He wept over disappointment in ministry (Luke 19:41-44). He was "sorrowful and troubled," "deeply grieved to the point of death"—so much so that he asked God for a release from his calling (Matthew 26:37-39). Under the stress of his ministry assignment, his sweat poured off him like great drops of blood (Luke 22:44).

As a pastor, God calls me to shepherd like Jesus—the great Shepherd of the sheep. I'm to lay down my life for the sheep. Teaching what is true may mean that I'm despised and rejected. Comforting people in suffering and death means familiarity with grief. And, of course, this calling is not unique to ordained pastors. Every believer in Christ is called to the work of ministry.

———

Luke 14 provides an excellent example of what ministry looks like. Jesus went to the house of a leading Phari-see to eat on the Sabbath. In front of his seat (perhaps arranged by his host) lay a man afflicted with a disease. The people scrutinized Jesus, watching to see what he would do (Luke 14:1). But what others might think of him didn't seem to matter to Jesus. Instead, he silenced his critics with a well-placed question and then healed the man. When others watch us, waiting to see if we will meet their expectations, we shouldn't fret. Instead, we should minister in the ways we can at that moment.

Jesus tells us not to scramble for approval and recognition (v 7-9). Instead, he teaches us to humble ourselves by taking the lowest place (v 10). In God's upside-down kingdom, he exalts the humble (v 11). Jesus practiced what he preached; that's why following him involves a cross (v 27). He humbled himself to the point where everyone despised him. He became a reject.

Humbling ourselves in miscarriage might mean exposing our condition. It may mean saying, "I'm not doing so well. I can't stop crying, and I'm overwhelmed with caregiving. I can't find it in myself to pray. I need help." It might mean being the sort of person that others don't want to be around: a burden.

That's the sort of humility that God exalts. Such humility serves your neighbor. Your friends may know what it looks like to help from a position of strength, joy, and beauty. But do they know what it means to serve from a place of weakness, sorrow, and ashes? That's how Jesus served us. Ministering from weakness may mean sharing about a sinful response or temptation during your sorrow, along with the grace you find in Jesus. It may mean testifying to Jesus' faithfulness when you are overwhelmed with doubt. Sharing your weakness shows others what Jesus is like.

———

First-century banquets were occasions to look good. When invited, you hoped for a seat of honor. When hosting, you invited guests who could return the favor.

It became a system for climbing the social ladder. But Jesus looks at the ladder and breaks its rungs.

He tells his followers not to use banquets to advance their social status. Instead, they should "invite those who are poor, maimed, lame, or blind" (v 13). He means that literally but also metaphorically: the parable in verses 16-21 points to the fact that, when his people Israel refused him, Jesus would send the gospel to the nations, like a man inviting outsiders into his house for a feast. Jesus invites the sinful, the spiritually dead, and the morally bankrupt into his kingdom. He humbled himself to invite the humbled to join him. He even calls us to join him in his humility (v 25-27).

In miscarriage, serving others may mean humbling yourself enough to speak honestly about your loss to them. They may know nothing of miscarriage. As you fold laundry or share childcare or ask for a lift to the hospital, you might find an opportunity to talk about your experience and what God is teaching you. Inviting them to see your grief may open their eyes to a wide range of experiences that God knows all about—giving them permission to admit their own struggles. You serve your neighbor by showing them that some problems don't have a quick or easy fix.

Serving others in our grief is following in Jesus' steps. We humble ourselves before others and invite them to join us. We may have less capacity than usual, and that's fine—but we needn't write ourselves off as useless in ministry. In fact, this may be a special opportunity to serve. We make space for those who are hurting—just as Jesus makes space for us.

REFLECT

- What makes you feel weak?
- Who could you minister to out of your weakness?

JOURNAL

22. LUKE 15

How Should I Care for My Other Children?

Our first and fourth miscarriages were so early in the pregnancy that we had told no one. The others, however, came further along. We had already told our children they were going to have another brother or sister. It was easy to announce the happy news; they were excited to meet each new arrival. But telling them that the baby had been miscarried was a lot harder. Each time, we were faced with the task of caring for our children through deep disappointment.

If you have children in the home, you might be wondering what the best way is to care for them. I can't give you a straightforward answer because there are significant variables in every situation. Your other children might be nine months old or well into adulthood—or anywhere in between. Each child has their own temperament. You may or may not have told them about the pregnancy. Every miscarriage is unique. All these things factor into a child's ability to understand and process what is happening, and into the way you should care for them.

But there is a key principle you can follow.

In Luke 15, Jesus encountered Pharisees and scribes who complained that he welcomed sinners (Luke 15:1-2). Jesus addressed their complaint with a series of three parables: about a man who loses a sheep (v 3-7), a woman who loses a coin (v 8-10), and a father who loses a son (v 11-32). What do these parables have to do with miscarriage and parenting? Each one features a collection of things that should be together. Sheep in a flock. Coins in a purse. A son in a family. You, too, have a "collection"—a family. You're responsible for the care of each member, as well as the whole.

(In a sense, this applies even if you don't have other children of your own. Who else forms part of your family? Your parents, siblings, nieces, nephews? Fellow church members? In this chapter I'm mainly addressing those who have children in the home, but even if that's not you, read on: I hope there will be encouragement and help here for you, too.)

Each of these parables features someone who cares about the things in their "collection." When something is lost, they long for its return. The man seeks the lost sheep. The woman seeks the lost coin. The father scans the horizon, seeking the silhouette of his returning son. Jesus' point is that God seeks the lost and rejoices when they are found. The Father is committed to seeing all his children together and safe.

As fathers, we should imitate God in our care for each member of the family. We're to seek their salvation through sharing about Jesus. We're to look for them when they're missing. We're to imitate the natural and commendable practice of caring and seeking. This includes helping our children to understand and believe gospel truths. If we see faith grow in them, we will rejoice with the Father.

Miscarriage offers an opportunity to tend to the spiritual life of your living children. It may be their first exposure to death—offering an opportunity to talk about sin and its consequences. As you or they weep, you can share about the Savior who wept over death and who died for us. You can speak of the hope you have through Jesus' resurrection from the dead.

That could apply to those aren't part of your biological or church family, too. Who do you have responsibility for or authority over? Who do you long to see welcomed into God's kingdom? This miscarriage, painful though it is, could provide opportunities for conversations about Jesus that always seemed impossible before.

———

Of course, each child will respond differently to the news. A small child might say to a neighbor, "Mommy had a baby in her belly, but the baby died. Do you want to see my doll? Her hair smells like peppermint!" An older child might retreat to his room or escape through activities or recreation. Another might hide in the closet to cry in secret.

Please do not wait for your children to come to you for care and attention. You're the father; they're the children. Seek them. Welcome their questions and their silence. Be patient with unusual behaviors and disobedience. Reflect on God's mercy and patience toward you and show them the same.

If your daughter doesn't know of the miscarriage, she may be wondering what happened to Mom. She doesn't understand why Mom and Dad are sad. Perhaps she thinks she's done something wrong and is afraid to come to you. Seek her out. Bring her into the safety of your embrace. Tell her what she needs to know using language she can understand. Invite her questions and answer them.

If your son does know about the miscarriage, he may experience the same questions, confusion, and feelings as you do. He wonders if it's ok that he wants to play in the baseball game tomorrow. Or he's embarrassed at his tears. Seek him out. Share that you're sad too and invite him to express his emotions. Let him know it is ok to cry or to laugh. A sad thing happened, but we're still in a world with happiness.

When something sad happens to the family, the child might fear for the family's future. So, at some point, gather your family to talk and pray. Let the children see that Mom and Dad love each other—and them. Show them that grief can be shared and discussed. Rejoice in God's goodness. *We're a family; we'll walk this road together.*

It's possible you'll find that your child cannot function at school, exhibits behavioral changes beyond a few weeks, or shows signs of depression or anxiety. In such cases, it may be wise to seek out an age-appropriate therapist. These professionals are trained in helping children understand and grieve loss. They'll offer you advice on how to help your child.

You have a heavenly Father who sought you and brought you into his family. Take some time to talk to him. Ask him to give you the wisdom to understand and know your children. Ask him to help you seek them and help them. He will help you. In fact, you might find he's been at work before you even asked.

REFLECT

- If you have other children, what are your hopes and prayers for each of them?
- How can you help them trust Jesus in this?

JOURNAL

(Focus verses: 19-31)

Can Anything Relieve
My Torment?

"Torment" means severe physical or mental suffering. As a man, it is unlikely that miscarriage would bring you lasting physical suffering. But intense mental suffering is entirely possible.

You may have dreamed of being a father since childhood. You looked forward to discussing your favorite novel with your son or working in the garden with your daughter. You planned to watch them in ballgames, see them graduate high school and college, and cry at their wedding. And then there might be grandchildren.

But the life you longed for hasn't come, because you've been unable to have children. With each miscarriage, the good things you desired seem to have vanished away. Meanwhile, to look out of your window is to see your neighbor playing football in the yard with his kids. Attending church means hearing children and watching parents grow exasperated over them—over these gifts from the Lord! Going to the store means hearing a child beg his mother for a candy bar in the checkout line. You wish you could buy your child one.

You don't want it to be so. You didn't choose this. But every time you see other people's children, you suffer mentally. You can't free yourself from it. "Torment" may seem like a label that fits. You wonder what can bring relief. Will it ever end?[5]

In our passage, Jesus tells the story of the rich man and Lazarus (a fictional Lazarus, not the one Jesus raised from the dead in John 11). In this story, two men—a poor man, Lazarus, and a rich man, who is given no name—both die. After death, their situations are reversed: the poor man becomes rich in comfort while the rich man finds only torment. This story offers us hope in our agony. As someone who trusts Jesus, you may put yourself in Lazarus's place in the story. Let's consider the parallels.

Lazarus suffered severely, being poor and covered with sores. You've suffered the loss of a child.

Lazarus longed for something good—the scraps that fell

---

5 If you suffer symptoms of anxiety or depression for longer than two weeks, I encourage you to see a licensed therapist for mental health care. They can also help you process your loss to prevent long-term mental effects. Or if you're in a depressive episode, they can help you to heal.

Our suffering is complicated because we are complex beings—body, mind, and spirit. Suffering can bring spiritual, mental, and physical trauma. Depression and anxiety may result from how our bodies, brains, and minds respond to a traumatic event. A pattern of thought shaped by the event may stick in our minds long after the event ends. A therapist should be able to recognize this and help you. Seeking mental health care is no different from seeking care for a broken arm. It is not a sign of spiritual weakness. It is good stewardship of the mind God gave you.

from the rich man's table. You see parents and children everywhere. You long for the good gift of a child.

Lazarus did not receive what he longed for. He was given no leftover food. Instead, the dogs came and licked his sores. You haven't received your child and become the parent you hoped to be. Instead, you've suffered loss.

Lazarus died without ever receiving the life he wanted. He never filled himself with the scraps that fell from the rich man's table. I don't know what your future holds. You may have a child; I pray you do. But it's possible you'll be like Lazarus in this regard, too. God does not promise us children. He does not promise us comfort, satisfaction, or safety in this life. His promises are far better than that.

Lazarus died and went to heaven ("Abraham's side"). "He is comforted here" (Luke 16:25). After a lifetime of receiving "bad things," he found relief in the presence of God. When you die, if you are trusting in Jesus, you will go to be with him—which is far better than anything on earth (Philippians 1:21-24).

Lazarus will never suffer torment again. The rich man, however, did not receive eternal comfort. He suffered anguish in hell, crying out, "I am in agony in this flame!" (Luke 16:23-24). He learns that a great chasm stands between torment and comfort—one that no one may cross. This chasm means that the rich man will never find relief from his torment. The opposite is true for Lazarus. Nothing—absolutely nothing—can end his comfort or bring him misery. Upon his death, he entered eternal joy and peace.

This story contains a grave warning: if, like the rich man, you place your hope in the things of this life, you will lose everything. But it also contains the ingredients to change our perspective on our earthly torment and find genuine hope—better hope.

If you trust God to forgive your sins through Jesus' life, death, and resurrection, then all that awaits you at death is joy. God has no anger toward you. He does not condemn you. Clothed in the righteousness of Jesus, you will be welcomed by God into his presence. One day he will resurrect you to live in an imperishable body—one that knows peace, wholeness, and satisfaction. "He will wipe away every tear from their eyes. Death will be no more; grief, crying, and pain will be no more, because the previous things have passed away" (Revelation 21:4).

It is important to grieve, as Lazarus would have done in the story. Your suffering is real and painful and it matters. At the same time, we must be sure to place our hope in the right thing.

Jesus, who cared so much about our suffering that he entered it and then rose from the dead, offers you endless comfort in his presence. He dwells in you already by his Spirit to comfort and strengthen you. And this is only a down payment on what is coming (2 Corinthians 1:21-22). One day we will be on Lazarus' side of the chasm. Separated from grief and agony. Eternally comforted.

Spend some time in prayer. Thank God for sending Jesus to suffer, die, and rise for you. Thank him for forgiving your sins and granting you eternal life. Ask the Lord to strengthen your faith. Plead for present relief and patience in suffering. Ask for the grace to remember and believe that Jesus is bringing you to something far, far better.

REFLECT

- What comfort do you long for?
- Do you believe that one day you will be completely cut off from torment?

JOURNAL

24. LUKE 17

What Do I Do Now?

I was twelve when my grandfather died. We'd spent several days at the hospital for the surgery. He died a few days later. Then there was time spent with family, a visitation, and a funeral at the church. For a week or more, life seemed to revolve around Grandpa's condition.

The funeral procession snaked through town from the church to the cemetery. Looking out of the car window, I was struck by how odd the world looked. People were working in their yards, running errands, going about life as usual. Everyone was oblivious to the fact that I had just lost one of the most important people in the world.

The next day, I had to return to school, do homework, interact with friends. How would I re-engage? What would I do? How was I to enter the "normal world" when my world had changed so significantly?

Life after a miscarriage can be like that. Your world had been one of anticipation, planning, preparing, and dreaming. Life with this child was very real in your mind.

And then, in one day, it vanished. For you, the world has completely changed. But for everyone else, it's as though nothing happened.

Maybe you've already returned to work, church, and the routine of "normal" life, but things feel slightly off. Perhaps you're disillusioned, wondering if anything in the world even matters. Or maybe this loss has been an awakening. You're dissatisfied with life as usual. You want to live for something more.

Wherever you're at, you face the question: what do I do now?

———

In Luke 17, too, there are two different worlds colliding. Jesus is showing both his disciples and the leaders of Israel how the way of the kingdom conflicts with the way of the world. Coming to faith in Jesus means understanding the world in a new way—and living accordingly.

In this chapter, we find four things we can do right now, based on that kingdom perspective. In what follows, I will skim the high points of the chapter. If you have time, I encourage you to read one section at a time, and then go back to Luke 17 and meditate on the corresponding passage before you go on to the next section. Or, after finishing the chapter, pick one point that struck you, reread the passage it comes from, and meditate on it.

———

1. *Tend to relationships (v 1-4)*. Stress and grief can be a strain on relationships. Seasons of loss threaten to end marriages and friendships. You've been short with the kids or impatient with your wife. Or she sinned against you, or a friend said or did something thoughtless, or the church showed little concern. You can't seem to move past it. If left unaddressed, bitterness will fester and threaten to destroy the bonds between you.

Jesus calls us to "be on [our] guard" against sin in our relationships (v 1-4). If your brother or sister sinned against you, address it. If he or she repents, offer free and gracious forgiveness. This also implies that if you've sinned against others, you need to confess your sin and express your sorrow to the offended person. Reaffirm your love for them and seek reconciliation. Jesus says it is better to have a millstone hung around your neck and be thrown into the sea than to cause one of his people to stumble, so deal seriously with sin. Don't allow one loss to lead to the loss of more.

2. *Keep serving Jesus (v 7-10)*. Jesus says that when a servant finishes plowing, he will not be invited to rest and eat. No, it's the servant's job to serve—and that means preparing the meal and waiting on the table. Servants serve until all the service is complete.

So, Jesus reminds us that we must keep serving him. It doesn't matter how much we've served in the past; we're to keep obeying him in the present. That doesn't mean we never get to rest—but it does mean that so long as we're living, Jesus has work for us to do. Whether you're full or empty, sorrowful or rejoicing, make it your aim to bring glory to our King.

3. Give thanks (v 11-18). In this passage, Jesus is traveling to Jerusalem. As he enters a village, ten men with leprosy stand at a distance, crying out to Jesus for mercy. Jesus sends them to the priests, and as they go, they are healed. But only one of them returns to glorify God and thank Jesus. Jesus commends this man's thankfulness.

In a time of grief, it's easy to overlook the ways that God has blessed us. God has saved us from our sins. He is making us more like Jesus. We can look at friends, family, church, career, and more as signs of God's goodness. Focused on our suffering, we become blind to how God is helping us. Our faith should give us eyes to see how Jesus loves us. We should return, glorify God, and thank Jesus.

Think back on the prayer requests you've made throughout reading this book. Has God answered some of them? If so, how? Who and what did God provide? How did he sustain you? The answers to those questions reveal God's kindness. Give thanks.

4. Set your hope on Jesus (v 20-37). You may wish to "return to normal"—but take care what that "normal" is. People went about their everyday lives in the days of Noah and Lot—and God's judgment took them by surprise. That is how it will be when Jesus returns in glory (v 26-35). We don't know when Jesus will return. But we know that he will. We should live like we are waiting for him.

The days and weeks following my grandfather's death

prompted me to think frequently about heaven and our resurrection. While it seemed that the world had moved on, I didn't. Yes, life returned to "normal," but I re-entered the old world a new boy. The world was the same, but my perspective was now better informed and bolstered by the promise of eternal life.

My prayer for you is that this season of grief will train your heart to understand that, while no happiness is lasting on this earth, the kingdom of God, which we have in Christ, goes on forever. In that sense, I pray you will re-enter your "normal" life a different man.

REFLECT

- Do you see the world the way Jesus sees it?
- What is one thing you will do today as a result of reading this?

JOURNAL

25. LUKE 18

Am I a Downer
to My Friends?

The labor and delivery wing of the hospital did not deliver meals to fathers in individual rooms. Instead, they provided a small self-service buffet during set hours in the hospitality room. Thinking nothing of it, I made my way there during the first mealtime of our stay.

I entered a room filled with a dozen other men waiting in line. These tired but happy fathers took turns asking about deliveries and babies' genders, exchanging congratulations, and sharing newborn pictures on their phones. Then one of them turned to me. "What about you? What did you have?"

My heart sank at the question, not merely because of our situation but because I knew what effect it would have on the room. Into this fraternity of enthusiastic joy, I would insert death and sadness. I stuttered through a quiet explanation. At once, the volume dropped. Smiles straightened; laughter was quieted. The energy in the room seemed to vanish.

Quickly, I turned the conversation to a question about another man's newborn, trying to fix it. But I felt horrible—Daddy Downer at their celebration. For subsequent meals, I waited until the last 15 minutes of the allotted time, always checking to see if the room was empty before entering.

I'm not alone in dreading being Daddy Downer. A few years ago, I wrote an article for Risen Motherhood, a ministry to moms, sharing about miscarriage from a father's perspective. In response, I've received a steady stream of messages from men who found it and resonated with its message. They are at a loss to know how to cope with a miscarriage and are surprised at how it affected them. They don't have anyone to talk to, and no one is reaching out to them. These messages often lead to a conversation helping them navigate their heart and circumstances.

One common struggle among these men is knowing how to act around their friends. They don't know how to respond to a casual "Hey, man! How are you?" They're a total mess inside, but they don't feel free to share. When they do share, they feel like a downer. And they don't want to be the one constantly introducing grief into their gatherings. They want to know what to do.

My usual response is to keep sharing. Pray for God to open others' hearts to your story. Whether in a group or one to one with a close friend, admit that you need to talk to someone. Explain how hard this loss has hit you and that you need someone to walk through it with you. Yes, it will sting if the response is less than compassionate. But it is worth it. Keep seeking until you find someone who will minister to you in your pain.

In Luke 18, we find three scenes in which Jesus shows us what saving faith looks like. Each demonstrates the importance of sharing our needs. The first is about a widow crying out for justice (v 1-8). The second is about a tax collector crying out for mercy (v 9-14). Jesus commends the widow for her faith—sharing her need with the only one who can meet it—and the tax collector for his humility—rightly understanding his situation and his inability to save himself.

In the third scene, the disciples rebuke people for bringing their infants to Jesus (v 15-17). But Jesus invites the children to come to him, saying that the kingdom of God belongs to those who are like little children. This is where the widow's faith and the tax collector's humility come together. An infant requires everything to be done for her, so she cries until her need is met. Likewise, we're to recognize our inability to save ourselves and cry out to God for help. Being like a little child means having faith like the widow and humility like the tax-collector—and it's these things that enable us to enter the kingdom of God. And if honesty about our weakness is the attitude we're to have with God, it is certainly ok to have that attitude with others.

———

Suppose your friends, family, or church do not have a culture in which people are honest about their weaknesses and need. In that case, your humility will teach them what it looks like to be a Christian. Jesus welcomed little children—those who could do nothing but ask for help. Unless we receive his kingdom like a small child, we cannot enter it (v 15-17). We're so weak that we can't be saved apart from God's work (v 24-27). It is those who humble themselves who will be exalted (v 14).

In our asking, we must be sensitive to our friends' capacities. God is the only one we can cry out to all the time about everything. Only he has the limitless wisdom, power, and love to care for us fully and meet every need. Our friends are not God. They do not have an unlimited capacity for carrying suffering and grief. Such ministry may fill their lives already. At some point, they must say no. Present your requests with grace, asking if they can help and, if not, who might be able to help. Listen to them, too—find out about the burdens they are carrying and the joys they are experiencing. Be sensitive to their needs as you ask them to be sensitive to yours. Rejoice with those who rejoice, even as you ask others to weep as you weep (Romans 12:15).

But don't be afraid to be persistent in seeking help. Don't fear weakness and need. Genuine neediness is nothing to be ashamed of; it's a prerequisite for following Jesus!

Stop and pray. Share your weakness and need with the Lord. Ask him to give you the strength to be weak. Remember that he wants to know your requests and to answer them.

REFLECT

- What needs do you have that only Jesus can meet?
- What needs do you have that a friend could meet?

JOURNAL

Have I Failed Jesus?

When she finished, the ultrasound technician told us that the doctor would be in shortly. We didn't need to be told. We could see it on the screen for ourselves—a motionless body, settled at the bottom of the uterus. Our second miscarriage.

Since the baby's body had not passed naturally, the doctor ordered a D&C. He invited me to sit next to my wife as he performed the procedure. At that point, I had witnessed labor and delivery four times with no problem. I wouldn't even be watching this; I'd just be holding her hand and facing her. Nevertheless, I began to feel nauseated. I moved to a chair at the back of the room, but even there, I began to feel dizzy and queasy. Anxiety filled me. I told my wife that I needed to leave and would be in the waiting room.

I found a seat far from others, hoping no one would talk to me and ask about our pregnancy. But instead of someone else talking to me, I began talking to myself. *What kind of a man are you? You left your wife alone in her suffering? What a wimp! Aren't husbands supposed to provide leadership, protection, and provision? You're a failure as a husband and as a man! Jesus must be so ashamed of you.*

How was I to interpret the words in my head? *Had* I failed as a husband and as a man? *Was* Jesus ashamed of me?

To answer those questions, we first need to distinguish between feelings of failure and actual sin.

They're not always the same. We should recognize, for example, that we're not responsible for what we cannot control. We can't control what our bodies will and will not feel. I could have stayed in the room, hoping the feeling would pass. But what if I had passed out, collapsed to the floor, and cracked my head open or vomited during the procedure? Would that have served my wife well? No, it would have increased her anxiety. It might have distracted the doctor during delicate surgery. Sometimes we serve others well by acknowledging our inabilities. The truth about that scene in the waiting room was that I *hadn't* failed. I hadn't sinned.

The feeling of guilt isn't always pinned on one specific failing. I felt a general sense of failure with each of our miscarriages. Somehow, I thought, I had failed to protect my wife and my child. *If I were a better man, a better husband, and a better father, I could have kept this baby alive.* That's a ridiculous idea, I know, but it was real and present nonetheless.

Do you feel that way? Ask yourself: have I actually disobeyed God here? If the answer is no, be comforted.

But don't let yourself off the hook entirely. There *are* times—more than I can count—that I have failed as a husband. Too often, my pride has tempted me to care more about what people thought of us than how my wife was doing. There were (and are) times when I put my own needs ahead of hers. I have failed to process the miscarriage with her or to encourage her to talk with a friend. Our 23 years of marriage have likely contained more failure on my part than success. What do I do with these sinful failures? What do you do with yours?

I find encouragement in Jesus' love for Jerusalem, seen in Luke 19:41-44.

Jesus had just told a story about a nobleman who entrusts his servants with his money, telling them to do business on his behalf while he is away (v 11-27). He returns to see what they have done, rewarding and punishing accordingly. In like manner, Jesus traveled to Jerusalem—God himself entering his own city—to see what his people had done with what he had given them. Though the crowds sang his praises (v 28-40), he would find his people abusing and misusing his house (v 45-48).

As Jesus approached Jerusalem, he wept over it (v 41). He wept because he knew the destruction that would come upon the city (v 43-44). He wept because he knew it was preventable. The people of Jerusalem had failed to grasp what would bring peace (v 42). The Messiah—God in human flesh—had visited them to save them, but they did not recognize him (v 44). If only they had recognized their God and Savior, they could have repented, received him, and had peace. But they failed. They failed, and they would be punished for it.

That thought might not seem comforting in our failings—but it *should* comfort us if we are trusting in Christ. The Son of God came to earth precisely because we fail. We fall short of God's glory and deserve the punishment that Jerusalem received—total destruction. But Jesus so loved his sinful, failing people that he would surrender his life for their sake. He would give his body for them, walking forward to the destruction of his flesh in crucifixion. The wrath of God for our sins would fall on his body, and he would die. His veins would be opened, spilling sacrificial blood to enact a new covenant.

As God's people today, we have got right what the people of Jerusalem got wrong. We recognize that God has visited us in the crucified and risen Messiah. We come to know that Jesus brings peace for all who repent and receive him. Jesus wept for Jerusalem, but he did far more than weep for us.

Talk to God about your failures. Whether they are due to your human finitude or your willful rebellion, tell him about the things that cause you to feel shame. Thank him for Jesus, who sees both your sin and your shame and loves you anyway. Thank him for sacrificing his Son to cleanse you and make you his own. Ask him for the grace to repent, believe, and find peace in Jesus.

REFLECT

- How do you think you have failed?
- What will you do to keep reminding yourself that you are made spotless in Christ?

JOURNAL

27. LUKE 20

Is There Any Hope?

How has miscarriage changed the way you think about eternal life? For me, each miscarriage increased my longing for the world to come. Every disappointment and loss reminds me that, as the writer of Ecclesiastes reminds us, life "under the sun" is a vapor, "a pursuit of the wind" (Ecclesiastes 1:14). There is no accomplishment, no happiness, no good thing in this world that we can grasp and keep. These come and they go. The most we can do—and what God calls us to do—is to remember him, obey him, and trust that he will set everything right in the end (Ecclesiastes 12:1, 13-14).

There is a good end for those who trust in Jesus—a new heaven and a new earth, where everything will be made new (Revelation 21:1-4). But not everyone has believed this. The Sadducees were a Jewish sect of wealthy, conservative leaders who denied a future resurrection of God's people, along with the existence of angels and spirits (Acts 23:8). In Luke 20, the Sadducees pose an absurd question to Jesus, perhaps hoping that he will also deny the resurrection. The Law of Moses protected Jewish widows and their late husband's estate by requiring that a brother-in-law marry her and produce offspring. The Sadducees tell the story of a widow married and widowed by seven brothers, one after the other. They ask Jesus who she will be married to in the resurrection—a resurrection, remember, that they don't believe in.

That question has some relevance to miscarriage and infertility. It echoes the questions about the coming age that plague us. *Will my miscarried children be there? If so, will they know us as their parents? We've never had children—will our life in the new world be "less than" those who had a quiver full?* It's ok to ask questions about what resurrection will be like, so long as we ask them in faith and acknowledge that we'll never answer them all in this life. What's vital is that we remember there is a resurrection— and that it will be glorious and free from sorrow.

Jesus demonstrates the pointlessness of the Sadducees' question by insisting that they don't understand the nature of the coming age. The Sadducees hypothesized that a resurrection age would be entirely like this one. But Jesus exposes this as a false assumption. The present age and the one to come are different.

In the resurrection from the dead, there is no marriage. As children of the resurrection, we cannot die. Since we cannot die, there is no need for reproduction to fill the earth. Therefore, there is no need for marriage, the institution within which God designed procreation to occur.

Marriage and family relationships between individuals will dissolve in the resurrection. That is not because such things are bad—they are good! But these good gifts, necessary in the present age, will give way to something better. The beauty and benefits of marriage and family will be fully and forever satisfied by our relationship with Christ and the family of God's people. It's hard to imagine this, but it's true—and it will be excellent.

It's right to mourn the loss of children. That isn't how God meant the world to be. And that pain may linger throughout the rest of our lives, coming and going in waves. But the day is coming when the pain will cease entirely. We will be healed thoroughly in the resurrection. On that day, we will see and be with Jesus in the truest sense.

———

Because the resurrection is so unimaginable, it is easy to relegate it to the informational side of our faith. We rarely marinate in it enough for it to soak into our hearts. But we should. Jesus makes the resurrection a foundational aspect of his message. It is to define our reality, and it helps us understand who God is.

Jesus brings God's identity into the debate over resurrection. He cites Scripture, noting that Moses "calls the Lord the God of Abraham and the God of Isaac and the God of Jacob" (Luke 20:37). It's not that the Lord was their God; the Lord is their God. That means they must still be alive: there must be life after death—eternal life.

Therefore, Jesus reasons, "He is not the God of the dead but of the living, because all are living to him" (v 38).

The Lord God gave us life, and the Lord identifies himself with the ongoing life of his people. Think about that! God raises us from the dead—that's integral to who he is! If our resurrection reveals who God is, how much more should it reveal who we are?! As believers in Jesus, our primary identity is as people who will live forever with God. Our life in this age is a relatively short, temporary aspect of our existence.

We should certainly cry out to God for help in this life. God will walk beside us in this world, just as he did with Abraham, Isaac, and Jacob. But that is only a foretaste of what is to come. Abraham, Isaac, and Jacob died in faith, without receiving what God promised them (see Hebrews 11:13). They lived in this world as "temporary residents" because they desired a better homeland and the city God had prepared for them (Hebrews 11:14-15). Let's learn to walk through every season of life with the faith of Abraham, Isaac, and Jacob—with hope set on our future and glorious resurrection.

REFLECT

- Has miscarriage changed the way you think about eternal life?
- How could you allow the resurrection to define your reality more?

JOURNAL

How Do I Cope?

How do you cope with suffering? My natural responses to pain range from railing against it to avoiding it altogether. Sometimes I become angry or irritable, thinking that an outburst will somehow make it go away. (It never does.) At other times, I try to ignore it, as though not acknowledging it will make it end. (It doesn't.) In between those two responses, I turn to distractions or devices to deaden the pain. That typically looks like immersing myself in movies or television shows, surfing the internet, or playing games on my phone. I use the temporary pleasure of these activities to numb the hurt.

The problem is that none of these responses help us cope. The Oxford English Dictionary defines "cope" as "to manage, deal (competently) with, a situation or problem." The responses I've listed above are a way of managing the suffering for a time. They are a distraction or a way of attacking it from a distance. Sometimes we need these momentary escapes—so long as they don't keep us from running to Jesus. But we should realize that none of these things fully deal with the situation.

As Jesus neared his death, he warned his followers of the dangers that would face them. There would come a time of destruction (Luke 21:5-6). False Christs would appear, bringing deception (v 7-9). Wars, natural disasters, famines, plagues, persecution, betrayal, and wrath would fill the earth (v 10-24). Sure enough, these events have typified life since the death and resurrection of Jesus.

During this age of difficulty, Jesus calls us to cope. Trusting God means putting your whole life in his hands, like the widow giving "all she had to live on" (v 4). Jesus tells his followers not to be alarmed but to be prepared to resist deception (v 8-9). We're to trust that Jesus will provide words and wisdom in adversity (v 14-15). We're to believe that, even if we die, God will keep us. We gain our lives only by the endurance of our faith (v 16-19). All these things are signs that he is returning for us very soon. Therefore, our Lord tells us, "Stand up and lift up your heads, because your redemption is near" (v 28).

———

Jesus doesn't mention miscarriage in these predictions. But neither does he list every single adversity to come. He doesn't mean to be exhaustive. Miscarriage is one of many different afflictions experienced between Christ's resurrection and his return. And, like the things Jesus does mention, it is an occasion for temptation, deception, and unbelief.

We live between having been saved by Jesus and experiencing the fullness of that salvation. In this age, our flesh is still weak and prone to temptation. "The devil is prowling around like a roaring lion, looking for anyone he can devour" (1 Peter 5:8). Satan doesn't care about your miscarriage. He doesn't give you a break because you suffered a loss. To him, it's an opportunity to take down injured prey.

In miscarriage, we face many temptations. We may be tempted to put our hope in false saviors. Adoption and some infertility treatments are good things—but if we pursue them in the belief that they will save us from our pain, we enter dangerous territory.

We're also tempted to dull our minds with worldly things. "Be on your guard," Jesus tells us," so that your minds are not dulled from carousing, drunkenness, and worries of life" (Luke 21:34). You may be tempted to throw yourself into partying and pleasure to cover the pain. Some will numb themselves with alcohol or drugs. Others immerse themselves in worry—allowing the anxious pursuit of children to be their all-consuming passion. These things dull our minds by taking our focus off the return of Jesus. They replace Jesus as our hope.

So how do we cope with these temptations in miscarriage? Peter says that we resist the devil by being sober-minded, alert, and firm in our faith, knowing that our suffering is experienced by believers everywhere (1 Peter 5:8-9). We're to be confident in Jesus as our Savior, even in our losses. I think Peter learned that from Jesus, from the things we read today.

Jesus says we should be on guard and "be alert" (Luke 21:34, 36). That means we are not surprised or alarmed by sufferings; we know they are necessary before Jesus returns (v 9). Preparation means trusting Jesus to provide what we need in every situation (v 14-15). We're not to believe that this miscarriage means Jesus failed us. We're to remember that all this brokenness—miscarriage included—points to the only genuine cure: to the return of Jesus. We're not to collapse and hang our heads in sorrow or shame. We should stand up and lift our heads, looking confidently for Jesus. That is what it means to be firm in our faith.

Our Lord tells his followers to do all this, "praying that you may have strength to escape all these things that are going to take place and to stand before the Son of Man" (v 36). Escaping temptation and enduring to the end in faith is not easy. In fact, it's impossible. Impossible without God's help, that is. Therefore, we pray and cry out for God's sustaining grace. The Father who gave his Son for us is happy to provide us with everything we need to keep believing (Romans 8:32).

Spend some time in prayer. Tell God about your weakness. Ask him to deliver you from temptation and evil. Confess your sin. Acknowledge the harmful idols you use to cope. Receive his forgiveness, given freely through Christ's death on your behalf. Remember that God is for you, committed to saving you. Ask him to give you the grace not just to cope moment by moment but to be firm in your faith and endure all the way until Jesus returns.

REFLECT

- In Jesus' warnings, what temptations are familiar to you?
- Which one of Jesus' instructions do you especially long to be able to obey?

JOURNAL

Is It Appropriate to Seek Pastoral Care or Therapy?

If I were asked to look back over 23 years of marriage and 20 years of pastoral ministry and identify my mistakes, there would be too many to name. But near the top of the list would be this: not seeking care for myself. On the face of it, that sounds selfish, but it's not. My failure to seek care for myself has underlain almost every way I've failed to care for others.

I thought that seeking care for myself was selfish in numerous ways. God called me to lead, teach, and care for others. Time spent tending to myself was a distraction from my calling. It would distract other pastors from their duties. Therapy would cost money. I'd be wasting time that I could devote to my family and church. But, looking back, I see that a bit of time seeking care for myself would have prevented me from wasting loads of time with others. Don't wait two decades to learn that lesson.

Look again at Luke 22:39-46. What do we see?

Jesus "made his way as usual to the Mount of Olives" (v 39), a place Jesus and his disciples retreated to often. He intentionally sought an opportunity for himself and his disciples to seek time out and care for themselves through prayer.

Jesus told his disciples to pray for themselves (v 40). He emphasizes the importance of this by waking them up and commanding them a second time to pray for themselves (v 45-46). Our Lord does not think it is selfish for his followers to pray for what they need—in this case, for protection from temptation.

Jesus prayed for relief from his suffering and devoted himself to his Father's will (v 42). He did not shrink from expressing his desire for the cup to be removed. But he put the Father's will first, submitting himself to it.

Jesus received the Father's care. As he prayed, "an angel appeared to him, strengthening him" (v 43).

In these verses, Jesus models the best kind of "self-care"—retreating to find strength from God in prayer. Christ demonstrates that it is not only acceptable to care for ourselves in this way; it is necessary. For Jesus to minister to us through the cross, he first retreated to seek his Father and was strengthened by the angel God sent. For the disciples to resist temptation, our Lord emphasized their need to retreat in prayer.

What comes to mind when you think of God's call to minister to others? Have you considered that part of your ministry is seeking care for your own body, mind, and spirit? A tow-truck driver won't be able to do his job for long if he doesn't tend to his own vehicle—filling the fuel tank, changing the oil, fixing damaged parts. Part of your ministry to your family and of your vocation and gifting is tending to your body, mind, and spirit. That means we seek spiritual, physical, and mental healthcare when parts of us are damaged or unhealthy.

Jesus' suffering encompassed the spiritual, physical, and mental. Our Lord certainly experienced deep spiritual anguish as he faced suffering the wrath of God on the cross. That had a mental effect—he was "in anguish" (v 44). It also affected him physically: sweat poured off his body like blood from an open wound. Suffering—even for the Messiah—is never so simple that it impacts only one aspect of our person.

Suffering is complex because we are complex; we have bodies, minds, and souls. Suffering brings both spiritual and physical trauma. So, don't be hesitant about approaching your pastor for spiritual care. Send him an email, make a phone call, or talk to him after a Sunday service. He will help you process your questions and point you to relevant passages of Scripture. He'll listen, weep with you, pray with you, and remind you of God's good promises in Jesus. Seeking proper pastoral care is good stewardship of the soul.

Depression and anxiety may result from how our bodies, brains, and minds respond to a traumatic event. Our minds may be stuck in thought patterns which are appropriate to the event itself but unhelpful as they persist beyond it. A therapist should be able to recognize this and help you. Seeking mental health care is no different from seeking care for a broken arm. It is not a sign of spiritual weakness. It is good stewardship of the mind God gave you.

Not everyone will require the help of a professional therapist. But all of us need to seek prayer, Bible reading, and people to pastor us. We need this just as much as we need to eat and sleep. It should be a fundamental part of our daily lives, whether we are having a particularly tough time or not.

Situations like miscarriage are opportunities to benefit from having someone coming alongside us and invest in us spiritually. This may be as simple as having a regular Bible study and prayer time with someone. It doesn't need to be complicated. Meet, read some Scripture, discuss it a bit, and pray. You don't necessarily need to be pouring out everything you're feeling, although that may indeed help. But you do need to be running to your Father in prayer. He's given you your spiritual community to provide personal support and to point you to himself, particularly in times like this.

Even when I acknowledge that seeking care is right, I still wonder if anyone will want to care for me. Won't I be a nuisance, going to caregivers with my problems? God is not annoyed with our requests for care; he commands them! If we are not a nuisance to God, we should not shrink back from bringing our genuine needs to others.

Jesus invites us to come to God in prayer. His example reminds us that God answers such prayers. What a precious gift! Why not go to him now in prayer? Ask him to show you what kind of care you need, to speak to you through his word, and to bring the right caregivers into your life.

REFLECT

- What do you find most moving in Luke 22:39-46?
- Who could you ask to care for you, and how?

JOURNAL

Is It Ok If We Decide to Stop Trying to Have Children?

After our fifth successful pregnancy, we decided to stop having children. Pregnancies had become increasingly difficult and destructive to my wife's body. Miscarriages had become more frequent. So, two years later, we were surprised to discover that my wife was pregnant again.

This pregnancy brought waves of clashing emotions. On the one hand, we had not planned for another child. On the other hand, we celebrate children as gifts from God, made in his image. We had not wanted another child, but we knew that we should want this child.

We reminded ourselves that God is sovereign. He gives good gifts to his children. We prayed for God to help us and thanked him for this baby. Soon, excitement grew in our hearts as we anticipated meeting our new child.

It was at that point that we learned that our new baby had died at five weeks. We hit another wall of emotions. Guilt over our grief upon learning of the pregnancy.

Grief over the loss of a baby we now desired. Relief, knowing my wife would avoid a burdensome and painful pregnancy. More guilt over feeling relief. Then the question of whether we were "done." If God had given us this baby, did he mean for us to have more? Was it ok to decide to stop trying to have children?

That last question can be difficult for those facing miscarriage and infertility. Miscarriage can be incredibly hard—physically, emotionally, relationally, and spiritually. It's especially difficult if you haven't had a pregnancy yet that hasn't miscarried. Perhaps you've reached the point of knowing that another miscarriage would be too much. You're willing to choose childlessness now. But in many churches, there are Christians who assume that all married couples should be having children. Some think it is wrong to avoid it intentionally. That brings questions: *Is it ok to stop? What will the church think? Will God understand?*

Many factors come into play in the decision to have children and how many. There is no passage in Scripture that speaks directly to your situation. We discern through snippets. There is a bit in Luke 23 that gives us help and hope.

As Jesus goes to his execution, he says a startling thing. A group of women are traveling with him, lamenting and mourning. Jesus turns and says, "Daughters of Jerusalem, do not weep for me, but weep for yourselves and your children. Look, the days are coming when they will say, 'Blessed are the women without children, the wombs that never bore, and the breasts that never nursed!'" (Luke 23:28-29).

The childless, *blessed?* When the Old Testament depicts an abundance of offspring as a blessed state? This was a shocking thing for Jesus to say. But he meant it. There are situations in which it is better to be childless.

These women were lamenting the imminent death of Jesus. But Jesus, knowing the future destruction of Jerusalem, tells them to weep for themselves. When judgment fell on Jerusalem through the hands of an evil empire, these women would envy those who had no children. Young children make it impossible to flee quickly, making families easy prey to invading soldiers. No mother wants to watch her children die or be raped and murdered before her eyes. And no parent wants to see a grown-up son go off to be killed in battle. "Blessed are the women without children, the wombs that never bore, and the breasts that never nursed!"

Jesus acknowledges something noteworthy here. He is aware of the hardships and anguish that having children can bring. He makes it plain that sometimes it is better to be childless.

———

There are other reasons too.

Consider the final instructions of Jesus. In creation, the Lord commanded the man and the woman to be fruitful, multiply, subdue the earth, and rule it. In the new creation, inaugurated in his resurrection, Jesus has brought that creation mandate to its fulfillment. He does not command his followers to multiply by having children.

Instead, Jesus' people are to multiply through evangelism, preaching the gospel to every nation (Luke 24:46-49; Matthew 28:18-19). Likewise, the way the earth is now to be subdued and ruled over is by proclaiming Christ's rule and teaching converts to obey what he commanded (Matthew 28:20).

The Great Commission fulfills the purpose of humanity. That is why Paul can write that it is better to be unmarried—and, this would imply, without children. Unmarried people are free to devote themselves entirely to the Lord (1 Corinthians 7:32-35). Childless Christians are free to spend more time investing in others. With fewer persons to care for in the home, they may be able to devote themselves to caring for those who have no one else to care for them. They may be more able to travel on short notice. Childlessness is *not* second best. In fact, Paul encourages singleness (and therefore childlessness) as his wish for all believers (1 Corinthians 7:7)! Blessed are the childless.

In this chapter, Luke brings us face to face with Jesus in his suffering and death. We find him unjustly accused, condemned, and sentenced to death. We see him mocked by soldiers and rejected by his people. We watch as he is crucified and dies. This is the Jesus we live for. He gave his all for us. He is worth devoting ourselves to entirely.

Spend time in prayer, asking the Lord for wisdom. If having children is not his will for you, ask him to satisfy that longing through your living for Jesus and to bless that living with kingdom fruit. Ask the Lord to show you if there is anyone to whom you could be a father in the faith.

Pray that he would lead you to persons without family that you could befriend and care for. Ask him to make you fruitful in ways you haven't yet imagined, even if he does not make you fruitful in this one way you have longed for.

REFLECT

- In what you have read today, what makes Jesus worth your devotion?
- What kind of fruitfulness will you ask God to bless you with?

JOURNAL

31. LUKE 24

"Peace to You"

Thank you, friend, for spending the past month with me. I count it a privilege to have a small place in your miscarriage story. I prayed for you often as I wrote this book.

I've prayed that sharing some of my experiences might help you realize that you are not alone. It helps to know that someone has gone before you, suffered what you suffered, and came through on the other side. I and many others have walked through miscarriage. It shaped us and changed us, leaving its mark on our lives. But it did not end us. We are still here—living proof of God's tender and patient love for fathers grieving a miscarriage.

More than my own story, I've prayed that sharing the story of Jesus would bring you hope and peace. It's easy to forget that Jesus was (and is!) a real human being. We've seen in Luke's Gospel how Jesus felt hunger and thirst, wept and felt sorrow, became tired and angry and troubled to death. His very real body was beaten and nailed to a cross, enduring significant pain. Real blood flowed from his wounds. Actual lungs breathed his last breath. A genuine heart stopped beating. It was this body that the women expected to touch and dress for burial when they arrived at the tomb. The life Jesus lived was as real as yours and mine. Being God in the flesh did not make life on earth effortless for Jesus. Life wasn't any easier for him than it is for you and me.

Jesus genuinely suffered. "They crucified him" (Luke 23:33). That short phrase speaks volumes, both physically and spiritually. Crucifixion was a form of execution designed to maximize and extend physical suffering. Spiritually, it signified a curse. "Christ redeemed us from the curse of the law by becoming a curse for us, because it is written, Cursed is everyone who is hung on a tree" (Galatians 3:13). Jesus' suffering was worse than anything any of us has experienced. He drank the cup of God's wrath for the sins of the world. That was no accident; it was "necessary for the Messiah to suffer" (Luke 24:26).

Elsewhere we are told that Jesus "had to be like his brothers and sisters in every way, so that he could become a merciful and faithful high priest" (Hebrews 2:17). He became like us *in every way*. There is nothing that we experience that Jesus didn't experience in some way. That means he can "sympathize with our weaknesses" (Hebrews 4:15). He knows what we are going through, and so he is merciful and kind to us.

Don't we see such a Savior in Luke 24?

"Peace to you!" Those are Jesus' first words to the Eleven after rising from the dead. He died and rose so that he might bless us with peace. The disciples think he is a ghost—a spiritual apparition, not the actual human Jesus. Knowing they are troubled and full of doubt, he acts to bring them peace. He offers his body to them, invites them to see that he is flesh and bone. He tells them to look at his hands and feet, which still bear the marks of crucifixion (see John 20:27). The Jesus standing in front of them is the very same man they watched die—alive.

It is one thing to read pieces of my story and hear how God has helped me. But I am dust, and to dust I shall return. I am perishing and will die. But Jesus is different than me. He went through the very worst and came through victorious. He died under God's wrath, and he rose from the dead.

Jesus is not simply a good example. He's not merely proof that you can, if you try hard enough, get through this. No, he's better than that. Jesus is the guarantee that his followers *will* get through this. He died our death so that we would rise in his resurrection. He lived our life so that we might live his—being remade into his image day by day, ready for future glory (Colossians 3:4, 10).

Jesus did it all for us. That's why he declared, "Peace to you!" when he first saw his disciples. That's why he raised his hands and blessed them as he ascended into heaven (Luke 24:50-51). He went through death and came back for our good.

Jesus died and rose to reconcile us with God. He opened our minds to understand that so that we would believe this (v 45). When we do, God forgives our sins, adopts us, transforms us, and guarantees that he will raise us from the dead with a resurrection like Christ's. Nothing can change that. Jesus sealed the agreement in his blood (22:20).

I don't know what lies ahead for you, friend. (I don't know that for myself.) But whether rejoicing or mourning, I pray you will look to Jesus in all things. The risen Savior holds out his scarred hands as proof that he's been where you are and came through on the other side. He's got this. Even better, he's got you.

REFLECT

- What peace have you found as you have read this book?
- How will you keep looking to Jesus now?

JOURNAL

Understanding the Medical
Side of Miscarriage
by Jenn Hesse

M iscarriage takes a toll on a woman's mind, spirit, and body. Talking to your wife about her emotions, while important, only addresses part of the pain. By learning about the medical aspects of miscarriage, you can honor the Lord and support your wife as you navigate grief together.

WHAT MISCARRIAGE MEANS

In medical terms, a *miscarriage* is the spontaneous loss of a pregnancy any time in the first 20 weeks after conception.[6] Most miscarriages happen in the first twelve weeks of pregnancy. The death of a baby at 20 or more weeks of pregnancy or during delivery is called a *stillbirth*. A woman who experiences two or more miscarriages is said to have *recurrent pregnancy loss*.

---

6 Medical definitions and most of the information in this article
come from Mayo Clinic (www.mayoclinic.org/diseases-conditions/
pregnancy-loss-miscarriage/symptoms-causes/syc-20354298,
accessed Sep. 27 2021).

Your wife might have realized something was wrong with her pregnancy when she started bleeding. Other signs of miscarriage include cramps, stomach and back pain, passing fluid or tissue through the vagina, and lessening pregnancy symptoms.

MORE WORDS TO KNOW

Miscarriage can be confusing, especially if you aren't familiar with medical terminology. Expect to come across these pregnancy-related words:

- *HCG:* Human chorionic gonadotropin, a hormone produced in a woman's body only during pregnancy. Pregnancy tests work by finding HCG in urine or blood.
- *Placenta:* An organ attached to the uterus and connected to the baby via the umbilical cord. The placenta provides oxygen and nutrients to the baby and removes waste from the baby's blood.
- *Embryo:* A baby in the early stages of development until nine weeks after conception.
- *Fetus:* A baby from nine weeks after conception until birth.

WHY MISCARRIAGE HAPPENS

Most miscarriages are due to genetic problems with the baby. In pregnancy, when a sperm fertilizes an egg, genetic information stored in chromosomes is passed from both parents to the baby. A baby with extra or missing chromosomes doesn't develop normally. Abnormal chromosomes can lead to...

- *Blighted ovum:* an embryo never forms.
- *Molar pregnancy:* both sets of chromosomes come from the father, instead of one each from the father and mother.
- *Partial molar pregnancy:* one set of chromosomes comes from the mother and two come from the father.

Pregnancy loss also happens in an *ectopic pregnancy*, when a fertilized egg implants and grows outside the uterus. The fertilized egg can't survive, and the growing tissue causes complications for the mother. To prevent life-threatening bleeding, health-care providers remove ectopic tissue using medication or surgery.

Your wife might be at greater risk for miscarriage if she has diabetes, thyroid disease, or uterus or cervix problems. Smoking, heavy alcohol use, and using street drugs also increase risk.

TESTS AND TYPES OF MISCARRIAGE
Health-care providers use several tests to diagnose miscarriage:

- *Pelvic exam* to see if the mother's cervix is dilated (opened).
- *Ultrasound* to check the baby's heartbeat and growth.
- *Blood tests* to check the mother's HCG levels.
- *Tissue tests* to confirm miscarriage and rule out certain causes.

If your wife has had two or more miscarriages, her health-care provider might order *genetic tests* for her and for you to see if chromosomes are an issue.

Tests show what type of miscarriage a woman is going through:

- *Threatened miscarriage:* She's bleeding, but her cervix hasn't dilated. Her pregnancy will probably continue without other problems.
- *Inevitable miscarriage:* If she's bleeding and her cervix is dilated, miscarriage is expected.
- *Incomplete miscarriage:* Some tissue from the baby or the placenta left her body, but some stayed in her uterus.
- *Missed miscarriage:* Pregnancy tissue stayed in her uterus, but the baby didn't survive past the embryo stage or an embryo never formed.
- *Complete miscarriage:* The baby and all pregnancy tissue left her body.
- *Septic miscarriage:* An infection developed in her uterus after the miscarriage.

TREATMENT

Sometimes the mother passes the baby and pregnancy tissue naturally. In other cases, the health-care provider might prescribe medication to speed the process.

When tissue remains or there are signs of infection, the health-care provider will perform a minor surgery called a D&C (dilation and curettage).

In a D&C, the health-care provider dilates the cervix and uses an instrument called a curette to remove tissue and clear the uterus. Because the woman will receive some form of anesthesia, she might need some time to recover from possible nausea or drowsiness. Other potential side effects of a D&C include cramping and light bleeding.

For late miscarriages, the health-care provider will induce labor to deliver the baby.

CARE AND RECOVERY

Miscarriage can take up to four weeks to progress on its own. If your wife is waiting for the baby to pass, prepare to coach her through labor.

Bleeding, cramping, abdominal pain, and hormonal surges are common after miscarriage. Your wife might need help with tasks she doesn't feel up to doing. Be aware she might go through a time of postpartum depression.

A woman can usually get back to normal activities once the bleeding stops. If she keeps bleeding and has fever, chills, and pain, she could be developing an infection and will need medical attention.

NEXT STEPS

Your wife's period will probably return in four to six weeks after the miscarriage. It's possible she could get pregnant in her next cycle.[7] If you decide to try conceiving again, talk to her health-care provider beforehand. Depending on the circumstances, she might be given...

- *Progesterone:* a hormone that helps an embryo

---

7 Pregnancy after miscarriage information obtained from WebMD (www.webmd.com/baby/guide/pregnancy-miscarriage#4, accessed Sep. 27 2021).

implant and grow in the uterus.

- *RhoGAM:* a medicine to prevent mothers with
  Rh-negative blood type from developing antibodies
  that could harm the baby.

Moving forward after miscarriage requires patience. Be gentle with your wife and yourself as you process your loss. Keep in mind that anything associated with trying to get pregnant again, including sex, could trigger anxiety and grief.

Because of Christ, you can grieve with hope. Look to him for restoration while you and your wife heal.

How to Grieve

by Brian Croft

At the end of 2000, my wife miscarried our second child. It was early. She was about 6 to 8 weeks along. I had lost a child I had never met, and I did not know how to grieve.

I was ill-equipped to walk through this unique suffering. I had not been taught how to grieve. I was certainly not prepared to grieve a significant loss that others would see as insignificant. I failed miserably to care well for my hurting wife and to personally embrace the grief that I now believe is essential for processing this unique kind of loss.

So, my aim in this appendix is not to point to myself as an example. Far from it. Rather, I speak out of the wisdom I gained and lessons I learned through our own pain.

Men, it is good and right to grieve. It is necessary when you lose a child, regardless of how early the loss came or how many well-intentioned friends, family, or church members dismiss it as insignificant.

Here are five suggestions I learned about how you can grieve in a way that is good and helpful.

EMBRACE THE SADNESS

Any loss brings sadness. The loss of a child through miscarriage is no exception. Many of us do not see sadness as a good thing, so we run from it. But sadness can be healing. It is the gateway to restoration as well as the path by which we connect with others through compassion and empathy. It doesn't need to be all-consuming; sadness can be held together with hope, as this book explores (see especially chapters 10, 12, 23, 27). It's also an important, often overlooked way in which we can be like Jesus—who was described as "a man of sorrows and acquainted with grief" (Isaiah 53:3, ESV).

REJECT THE TEMPTATION TO MARGINALIZE

People mean well. They do. But many well-intentioned people marginalize the loss of a baby in the womb. This is especially true when a baby is lost in the first trimester. There's no visible baby. There wasn't even a noticeable bump. What's the big deal?

As men, we don't experience any of the physical symptoms and hormonal swings that often accompany a miscarriage. For that reason, we can be tempted to think that those who tell us this is no great loss are right. But they are not right. If this loss is a big deal for you or for your wife, accept it as such. Reject the temptation to be convinced otherwise.

SHARE YOUR GRIEF WITH OTHERS

My father was a general-practice physician for 45 years. He delivered approximately 3,000 babies throughout his career. So, his advice held a lot of weight with me when it came to pregnancy. His advice was not to share the big news with many until we got past the first trimester, just in case a miscarriage happened.

At first, when my wife miscarried, we were glad we followed his advice. We didn't have to go through the pain of tracking back and remembering all the people we'd told about the pregnancy. But what we learned was that it was even more painful to share about our miscarriage with those who had not known we were expecting.

The important thing is to be able to freely share your grief. Perhaps, like us, you wish you had told more people about the pregnancy. Perhaps you feel you told too many people. Whichever, it will be important to find at least one or two people with whom you can freely grieve. Not everyone will know how to respond or hold that space of grief for you. But find someone with whom you don't have to hold back.

MARK YOUR LOSS

In the same way that some people will marginalize the loss of your child, some will also not understand some of the steps you and your wife will need to take to grieve it. Nevertheless, do what you must. Marking your loss will help you to process it. Have a memorial service or funeral if you desire. Have a symbolic burial if you feel it would help. Talk about it freely with others or with just a trusted few. Post your thoughts and feelings on social media if you would like to. Do whatever you must do.

You and your wife are each unique human beings who just experienced a most devastating loss. Give yourself to the grief that you need to walk through, regardless of whether others understand. Only you will know what you need to do to grieve.

But whatever you do, do it together.

REMEMBER THE LOSS, ALWAYS

Many years later, I had stopped thinking about the miscarriage. But I noticed that my wife had not. She taught me this lesson: remember the loss, always.

We had a son before we lost our second baby. Then we had three more healthy children who have grown up and have been an incredible blessing. Surely enough time has gone by. Surely experiencing a full family life with multiple children fills that once-empty space of grief for that tiny child lost long ago? Not necessarily. Allow your wife to remind you of this, as mine still does.

———

Dear brother, embrace the grief. You are a man who lost a child. Be sad with your wife. Share it with others however often you need to, and however privately or publicly you want to. No one gets to tell you how to grieve your loss. No one except the man of sorrows who is acquainted with grief. And I have a sneaky suspicion what he might say.

Loving Your Wife:
Nate's Story
by Nate Wilbert

Above the bed was a branch, hanging horizontally from a string wrapped around both ends and looped over a nail in the wall.

This is what comes to mind when I remember the first miscarriage we went through, just months after being married: this branch of driftwood that Lore had found before we met. The bed was where we lay that morning when she came home after leaving work, after the miscarriage in her office bathroom. It's where my wife, who doesn't easily cry, wailed as I could do nothing but pray and hold her. And it's where we let go of names we'd attached to a face we hadn't seen.

Her entire being was in pain, and at least part of me sought an oblivion filled with trite words and fake smiles and distance. That was an old version of myself—the version I had wanted to leave behind when we married.

———

There's a recovery program at the church we used to attend. Men and women gather during the week to sing, read Scripture, and share testimonies of God's faithfulness. This was the first place I'd been where every week people spoke about God's faithfulness in the context of marriage difficulty, drug addiction, abuse, mental illness, grief, and on and on.

I started attending in an attempt to fix my first marriage. I figured I'd go for a month, learn what levers to pull, what buttons to push—and then my wife would understand how much I loved her. But I was in that room with other men for nearly three years: half the time separated, heading toward divorce, and trying to find Christ in the midst of it; and half the time divorced, lamenting, and trying to point other men to Christ.

I share this because one of the lessons I needed to learn, which helped prepare me for our miscarriages, was how to be more intimate with my wife. I'm not talking about sex. I'm talking about emotions, empathy, and engagement. My first wife and I tried very hard to have children. After several years without a baby, and after treatments that took a toll on her mind and body, we stopped trying. I told her it was going to be ok, and I never brought up the subject of children again.

I thought it was enough to have just that one conversation and stop the treatments and the scheduled sex. I missed an opportunity to pursue her in a way that showed care for her both as a bearer of God's image and as my wife. By the time I understood that she had never stopped thinking about having children, it was too late. And it was only when my first marriage ended that I realized a deep part of me still wanted a child.

———

Lore and I have also been unable to have children. Our miscarriage months into marriage was the first of many. Perhaps the low point was an ectopic pregnancy that sent Lore into the hospital for a week, brought prayers from all over, and opened my mind to what I imagined God could do. What I still imagine God can do. Just not what he did in our case.

In our case it seems we regularly miscarry. We're older. It's only been in the last year or so that I've accepted we might not raise a biological child. Talking about this with my wife, with other men and women, and with a counselor has helped. Sometimes I feel guilty because we haven't pursued adoption. Other times that clearly feels like I would be forcing something that God hasn't given me peace about.

One of the areas I work hard at in our marriage is avoiding passivity. I want to avoid some fantasy oblivion— an unhealthy make-believe world where I pretend that ignoring problems makes them go away. That's my struggle. Your struggle may be different. Perhaps it's numbing the pain through addictions, or perhaps other attempts to control your circumstances. Maybe it's the perpetual belief that if you could just find the right person...

Whatever it is, we're called to continually check the fruit of our lives against the fruit of the Spirit.

For me, there are several areas I try to work on, which I gleaned from leaders and friends in our recovery program. Trying to remember these areas in our marriage helps me prepare for the low points, like miscarriage, that regularly come.

Emotions: I ask my wife how she's doing. When I see that she's upset, I ask her what's wrong and press in even if she fakes being happy. At this point I can usually tell, and it's up to me whether I choose to pursue her or not.

Empathy: I am not my wife. I don't have her body. I have not lived the life she's lived. But I can ask questions and listen and use my imagination to try and draw closer.

Engagement: I'm not inclined to physical touch, but she loves to be touched. I give her hugs. I rub her feet when we watch a show on the couch. I hold her hand when we go for walks or grocery shopping or just sit watching the North Country sky.

Finally, I want to practice *embracing grace.* I pray for my wife, both with her and when I'm on my own. In addition to simply being present in whatever way she needs me, I have found prayer to be life-giving and hope-instilling during difficulty like miscarriage. It is a grace from our God.

I go through seasons in my spiritual life, so please don't misunderstand me: I'm not an expert at this. At times I struggle to pray, read Scripture, or go to church. As I write these words during a pandemic in a new town, all three are a struggle. However, I still believe there is grace from God in each of these acts—especially in community and the shared memory of Christ's sacrifice seen in taking bread and wine together.

The branch is no longer above our bed. Our bed now is not our bed then. But our marriage has survived. We are in a beautiful place discovering God's mercies. In Scripture. In the land and the people around us. In the vocations he has blessed us with. Even in the miscarriages.

Acknowledgments

This book would not exist without the help and encouragement of many co-laborers.

The Good Book Company: Thank you for grasping the vision for a miscarriage resource designed for grieving men and taking a chance on this book.

Katy Morgan: You are an excellent editor and delight to work with. I know it is cliché, but you really have made this a better book.

Jenn Hesse, Brian Croft, and Nate Wilbert: Thank you for sharing both your expertise and your stories with our readers. Many will be helped and blessed by you.

Jenny: This book came out of our sorrow, which was painful to walk through and is sad to talk about. Thank you for encouraging me to write this book and gladly providing space, time, and support throughout the process. I love you.

Jesus: You have walked with me through many sorrows. You've seen my weakness, fears, failings, and sin—but you've never left me or forsaken me. I couldn't ask for a better friend. I love you.

COMPANY

BIBLICAL | RELEVANT | ACCESSIBLE

At The Good Book Company, we are dedicated to helping Christians and local churches grow. We believe that God's growth process always starts with hearing clearly what he has said to us through his timeless word—the Bible.

Ever since we opened our doors in 1991, we have been striving to produce Bible-based resources that bring glory to God. We have grown to become an international provider of user-friendly resources to the Christian community, with believers of all backgrounds and denominations using our books, Bible studies, devotionals, evangelistic resources, and DVD-based courses.

We want to equip ordinary Christians to live for Christ day by day, and churches to grow in their knowledge of God, their love for one another, and the effectiveness of their outreach.

Call us for a discussion of your needs or visit one of our local websites for more information on the resources and services we provide.

Your friends at The Good Book Company

thegoodbook.com | thegoodbook.co.uk
thegoodbook.com.au | thegoodbook.co.nz
thegoodbook.co.in